Buyer Beware

Buyer Beware

The Hidden Cost of Labor in an International Merger and Acquisition

Elvira Medici and Linda J. Spievack

BEP BUSINESS EXPERT PRESS

Buyer Beware: The Hidden Cost of Labor in an International Merger and Acquisition

Copyright © Business Expert Press, LLC, 2017.

First published in 2017 by
Business Expert Press, LLC
222 East 46th Street, New York, NY 10017
www.businessexpertpress.com

ISBN-13: 978-1-63157-598-3 (paperback)
ISBN-13: 978-1-63157-599-0 (e-book)

Business Expert Press Business Law Collection

Collection ISSN: 2333-6722 (print)
Collection ISSN: 2333-6730 (electronic)

Cover and interior design by Exeter Premedia Services Private Ltd., Chennai, India

First edition: 2017

10 9 8 7 6 5 4 3 2 1

Printed in the United States of America.

Abstract

Recent years have seen a huge growth in European cross-border mergers and acquisitions (M&A), and considerable attention has been given to how such deals arise and are completed. A U.S. investor must understand the basic difference in the principle of individual labor law in the United States and how it compares with the laws of the target country in an M&A. The European Community's Directive calls for a cooperative relationship between employer and employees. Most theoretical emphasis has been placed upon noncultural factors although it is increasingly recognized business performance cannot be separated out from national or regional cultural influence.

In the United States, under the employment at-will doctrine, the U.S. private sector employers can dismiss their nonunionized employees at any time for any reason or even no reason at all. Thus, nonunion U.S. private employers do not have to demonstrate "just cause" to terminate an employee without paying severance or providing notice. They just have to make sure that the termination is not for discriminatory (e.g., based on sex, age, race, national origin, religion, or disability) or retaliatory reasons, which are outlawed by federal, state, and sometimes, local statutes.

In most European Union (EU) countries and Germany and Italy specifically, employees are presumed to have a basic right to keep their jobs indefinitely. One of the greatest labor cost disparity with the United States is not wages. It is the amount of paid time-off and other perquisites or benefits. Employers in Germany and Italy will find it difficult to discharge employees without incurring substantial liability. Termination without consequence to employer can happen only if the employer has "just cause." What constitutes "just cause" is often specifically defined in the law and nothing less than serious misconduct qualifies. If the employer cannot prove "just cause," it must either provide a lengthy pretermination notice period or pay a very generous severance based on seniority. For high-level, long-term employees, these severance payments can run into six or even seven figures. In addition, back wages often accrue until a ruling is made in the case.

The fundamental distinctions between these countries and the United States will not only influence a company's bottom-line profit, but also the success or failure of a merger and acquisition. These systems of corporate governance may come into conflict with American business' perceptions of what constitutes paid labor benefits and the need for "soft due diligence" research at the reacquisition stage. To assure success of the merger or acquisition or both and avoid a point of conflict, the company needs to understand the cultural landscape of the market, the target country's labor laws, investigate the cost of compliance or violation, and the success of the postacquisition phase.

Keywords

classification, employee rights, EU directive, FMLA, government regulations, international labor laws, istituto nazionale di previdenza social (INPS), labor counsel, maternity leave act, merger and acquisition, mutterschutzgesetz, parental leave, schutzfrist, termination, union, WARN ACT

Contents

Acknowledgments

A very special thanks to Professor Jeffrey A. Van Detta for his guidance throughout the process of writing this manuscript and Mary Wilson in helping us research this book.

We want to gratefully and sincerely thank Elena Ghigo of Johnson and Johnson International Italy Division and Edel Revord, HRM/T Organizational Development Mercedes-Benz, U.S. International, Inc. each provided an understanding and an intuitive insight into the actual customs and conditions affecting American corporations in foreign countries.

Linda—I would like to thank my family for supporting me through this new adventure and encourage my grandchildren to never let anyone or anything stop them from pursuing their dreams. And to a very special woman, colleague, and friend, Elvira Medici, who continually pushes me to be better.

Elvira—I wish to thank my family for supporting me in my decision to continue my education. I want to thank my special friend and associate Linda Spievack for encouraging me to obtain my LLM and then burning the midnight oil with me in researching this book. Special thanks to my husband Giorgio Medici for his patience and encouragement to pursue my dream of becoming an author.

Introduction

In today's global economy, corporate mergers and acquisitions (M&As) have become a part of economic reality. Increasing competition from foreign corporations and a general downturn in economic conditions have caused many United States companies to look for innovative methods of establishing a competitive presence in international markets. Globalization opens many U.S. companies to a broader outlook of an interconnected and interdependent world, with free transfer of capital, goods, and services across national frontiers. The synergistic gains from M&As may result from more effective and efficient management, economies of scale, more profitable use of assets, exploitation of market power, and the use of complementary resources; yet, results of many empirical studies show that many M&As fail. Perhaps, part of the reason for the failure is rooted in what drives most businesses—the intangible element of "human capital," and the culture reflected in performance levels.

Until recently, American courts, legislatures, employers, and unions have viewed our labor relations system as the "only reality". Consequently, little interest has been shown toward the labor laws and practices of other countries. With an increasing focus on foreign labor-management relations as a way to increase productivity in American corporations, many labor law specialists have examined the various labor-management systems that exist in other industrialized countries. It has come as a shock to many of our labor law specialists to learn that some features of our system, far from exemplifying the international norm, are regarded by foreign observers as anomalous, if not downright peculiar.

In reality, sometimes, the nearest a management group gets to understanding the dynamics of a newly acquired business is opening the books on day one after the acquisition or merger routinely as a direct result of the confidentiality of management information during the acquisition. While the management must give the supervisory board unlimited access to information, the board members, in turn, must keep the information secret, until the acquisition or merger is complete.

The book will concentrate on shedding light on important differences in international labor law between United States and specifically Germany and Italy and provide a process for the American labor lawyer and American investor to evaluate international labor and employment laws that regulate and impact foreign corporate governance, labor relations, bottom-line profit, and eventually, success or failure of the international merger and/or acquisition.

CHAPTER 1

Due Diligence: Scrutiny of Labor Law of Target Countries (Germany and Italy) in Relation to U.S. Labor Laws

Distinction in Terms: Labor Law and Employment Law

The U.S. term "labor and employment law" does not translate easily because of differences in language and usage between the United States and the multilingual European Union (EU). In the United States, there is a distinction between "labor law," which relates to unionized workers and collective bargaining and "employment law," which relates to equal employment issues and to employment issues of nonunionized workers. This distinction does not exist in EU countries. Generally speaking, the European term "labor law" covers all laws relating to employment.

Distinctions in Legal Regulations

In addition, the distinction between regulated and unregulated aspects of industrial relations and human resources cannot be drawn sharply for a supranational body such as the EU. Items that are subject to legal regulation in the United States, such as union recognition and the collective bargaining process, may not be subject to legal regulation in a particular EU country. Likewise, items that rarely are regulated in the United States, such as whether employers must give private sector employees time off for holidays, may be determined at a minimum level in EU legislation and in a more detailed fashion in individual Member States, where a higher standard of employment protection may be maintained or introduced. The EU has acted to harmonize laws in the labor and employment "area," which should be understood to indicate that in some countries, the issue may already have been the subject of legal regulation, while in other countries, it might previously have been unregulated. The term "harmonization" does not equate with unification. It is a flexible term designed to achieve, where necessary through binding EU legislation, a greater degree of similarity between laws, but not a uniform system of labor and employment regulation.

Protective Legal Framework of Social Policy

The EU, in response to factors such as technological progress, globalization of trade, unemployment, and ageing population, introduces a protective legal framework for the European citizens. This protective legal framework was named "social policy." The term "social policy" is used generically in the EU to encompass all forms of workplace regulation, including health and safety systems, equality laws, dismissal protection, worker involvement in decision making, and more broadly, job creation programs, education, vocational training, public health, and social welfare policies. In most areas of social policy, legal authority for regulation lies with the Member States, which determine the overall structure of their social systems. EU labor and employment laws are intended to be supplementary and must be sufficiently flexible to be compatible with the range of social systems operating in the Member States.

Definition of Worker and Employee

Another difference in terminology relates to the term "workers," which, in the United States, implies blue-collar workers, with the term "employees" having a more neutral connotation. This is not the case in Europe. U.S. practitioners reading the term "workers" in European materials should bear in mind that this means all employees, including casual workers. When the term "employees" is used in EU legislation, individual Member States may limit coverage to those who have a contract of employment, as determined by national law. The U.S. distinction between exempt and nonexempt employees is virtually unknown in Europe. In the United States, this distinction is based on classifications made in the Fair Labor Standards Act (FLSA), which, as a general rule, exempts from coverage those performing managerial or creative work.

Distinction Between Workers and Employees in Reference to the Public and Private Sector

In addition, the laws of most EU Member States and the directives of the EU make no distinction between private sector and public sector workers. Thus, if a directive applies to "workers," it normally applies to persons employed in both publicly and privately owned enterprises. However, where an EU directive refers only to "employees," a Member State may exclude civil servants with a public-law status who are deemed to fall outside the coverage of national employment law. Within the public sector, the term "civil servant" has a rather vague meaning in the United States, and often may be used to refer to anyone who is employed by the government. In Europe, civil servants are more narrowly defined; the term generally refers to persons who carry out the policymaking functions of the state or who have some influence on those functions. The question of who is a civil servant has not been much of an issue in the EU. The litigated question has been what circumstances permit a Member State to exclude civil servants from the coverage of a directive.

The Due Diligence Process and the Regulatory Compliance with Labor Law Provisions

When a company begins to consider mergers and acquisitions (M&As), the typical due diligence includes asset valuation, historical and future earnings valuation, comparative valuation, discounted tax flow, tax consequences, and legal structures. More companies are beginning to understand that culture plays a role in determining the success or failure of an international partnership. Understanding a potential partner's corporate culture and national culture can mean the difference between success and failure of M&As. While commercially sensitive information cannot be exchanged prior to a merger or acquisition, the legal and integration team of the acquirer needs to conduct the due diligence in the area of regulatory compliance and clearance, including timing issues. Despite globalization of business across national frontiers, labor is not interdependent and cross-border. It is imperative to investigate the labor and employment law provisions in the target country particularly because labor and employment interpretations in many foreign countries are subject to frequent reforms and revisions by the legislature and the courts. These reforms and revisions significantly affect and influence the existing employer–employee relations. The acquirer needs to be aware of the entire employment law spectrum of the territory from the beginning of the employer–employee relationships to notice of termination, mediation, arbitration, and litigation, as well as termination agreements, regulations concerning industrial relations, work agreements between employers and staff representatives, and collective agreements between employers and trade unions. In the event that M&As will require changes in the company structure, the following information must be investigated as part of the initial due diligence effort: the law on work committees, the law concerning written cautions, the law on labor leasing, regulations concerning executives, M&As, and possible sales and shutdowns of companies and all relevant labor law consequences.

The Cooperative Employer–Employee Relationship

It is important to note that, in the United States, the employer–employee relationship, as established by the National Labor Relations Act (NLRA), still has an adversarial connotation, while in Germany and Italy, the relationship is cooperative. Three primary mechanisms of worker participation exist in Germany: (1) collective agreements negotiated by trade unions, (2) workshop codetermination by way of works councils, and (3) supervisory board codetermination. Italy is a founding member of the EU, having cosigned the Treaty of Rome on March 25, 1957. Italy is subject to EU directives and regulations and to the decisions of the European Court of Justice. The following are the relevant EU directives implemented in Italy: (1) European Works Council, (2) collective redundancies, (3) transfers of undertakings, (4) workplace safety, and (5) free movement of workers. This information is significant to a U.S.

Corporation that may be considering an M&A because the cooperative attitudes in EU, and especially, Germany and Italy have strong statutory underpinnings and are embedded in wider employee relations systems that recognize the interests of labor. For example, under German labor law, employers with more than five employees have a statutory duty to establish works councils at the request of employees, which then have a range of information rights (covering financial matters), consultation rights (covering, for example, workforce planning, working environment, job content, and the adoption of new technology), and codetermination (joint decision-making) rights (covering "social" matters including the principles of remuneration, [PRP], work schedules, overtime, holidays, recruitment, and dismissal). The U.S. employer must shift from the adversarial to cooperative mentality in order to secure a successful merger or acquisition.

CHAPTER 2

Comparative Analysis of the At-Will Employment Concept and Doctrine in the United States and Related Employments Laws in Germany and Italy

Many U.S. companies due to the adversarial mentality and the influence of the at-will employment environment will be shocked to find out how much time and money will be required to accomplish a reduction in force or an involuntary separation for cause in Germany and Italy due to their applicable labor protections statutes, collective bargaining agreements, relations, and cultural attitudes. The Employment-at-will Doctrine (EAWD) provides that, absent a legal rule to the contrary, either party to an employment relationship for an unspecified term can terminate the relationship for good reason, bad reason, or no reason at all, despite the employee's length of service, with or without cause or notice, and without giving any explanation or reason, unless the freedom to terminate is constrained by contract. "Conversely, where employment is for a definite term based on a contract, an employer can terminate only for cause." The modern interpretation of EAWD recognizes that the employer's freedom to terminate at-will can be, and often is, restrained by statutory employment standards or limitations of the common law; however, the relationship between employer and employee remains unbalanced. The courts dealing with challenges to at-will presumption have carved out exceptions to mitigate EAWD's sometimes harsh consequences. The three major common law exceptions are public policy, implied contract, and implied covenant of good faith. The at-will presumption remains strong, and it can be difficult for an employee to prove that the challenged circumstances fall within one of the exceptions. Under the EAWD, the presumption is that the employee is only a supplier of labor who has no legal interest or equity stake in the business other than the right to be paid fair wages for labor performed, while the employer, as the owner of the business, has the sole right to determine all matters concerning the operation of the business. U.S. companies that are contemplating mergers or acquisitions of companies in the European Community (the "EC" or the "Community") must take into consideration the Directive of EC as well as the strict regulations of the Member States, which aim to protect employee rights and increase job security. The EAWD concept is odd in the EU community, and violations of the EU Directive and the Member State employment protection regulations can become costly in terms of time. In contrast to the free-wheeling EAWD, the EU countries have specific statutory schemes that address termination of employment, as demonstrated in the next subsections.

The German Employment Law Provisions

The German law contains a complex set of mandatory notice provisions for the termination of employment contracts and relationships. One requirement for an effective termination is the legally effective service of a notice of termination. Pursuant to Section 623 of the BGB Civil Code, a notice of termination must be in writing to be valid. A specific recitation of the reasons for termination is usually not necessary in the notice of termination (although, as an exception, reasons are required for contracts with apprentices and other training contracts). Another formal point is that any termination notice should be issued by one or more officers or directors who are registered as company representatives in the commercial register. If the termination notice is signed by another employer representative who has not been designated toward the employee as having authority to give notice of termination, the employee can reject the notice without undue delay if it was not accompanied by the original of a power of attorney for the signatory and the employer must give notice again.

In analyzing the applicable notice period provisions, one first looks to the applicable collective bargaining agreement (if any). A collective bargaining agreement could control by virtue of the parties being directly bound by the agreement, by virtue of their having incorporated the terms by reference into the employment agreement, or by virtue of a government declaration of general applicability. In all such instances, the collective bargaining provisions with respect to termination notices preempt any statutory termination notice provisions. Section 622, Paragraph (4) of the BGB Civil Code expressly specifies that the statutory notice periods can be superseded by the notice periods contained in a collective bargaining agreement, and that the notice periods in such collective bargaining agreements can be longer or shorter than the periods required by Civil Code, Section 622(1) to (3). The only restriction is that it is unlawful to agree upon a longer period of termination notice for the employee than must be given by the employer. Under Section 622(1) of the Civil Code, there is a general requirement to give notice of termination of four weeks, effective as of the 15th of the month or the end of the month, where more specific provisions, do not apply.

There is a general protection against (ordinary) termination of the employment relationship embodied in the Termination Protection Statute of August 25, 1969. If an employment relationship falls within the scope of the Termination Protection Statute, then the termination is only possible under the limited terms of that law.

An employment relationship falls under the Termination Protection Statute if both of the following requirements are met: (1) the employee must have worked for the same employer for more than six months without interruption and (2) the employer must, in the ordinary course, employ in an operation in Germany more than ten employees (excluding apprentices and trainees). Part-time employees with a regular weekly working time of no more than 20 hours are accounted for with a factor of 0.5, and those with a regular weekly working time of no more than 30 hours with a factor of 0.75.

A U.S. company considering a merger or acquisition or both in Germany must be aware that any postmerger restructuring plan that may require some layoffs will result in a lengthy and expensive process because employee wages and benefits must continue through the required notice period under the Termination Protection Statute.

The Italian Labor Law Provisions

Under the Italian law, the dismissal of employees is subject to stringent restrictions. Employers cannot dismiss employees at will, and mere labor-saving dismissals are not allowed. As a matter of fact, employees can be lawfully dismissed only in the presence of a "just cause" or "justified grounds."

- *Giustacausa* (i.e., just cause), means any serious breach that renders the continuation of the employment impossible, including, for instance, theft, riot, and serious insubordination and any other employee's behavior that seriously undermines the fiduciary relationship with the employer.
- Justified grounds means either (i) a less serious breach by the employee (e.g., failure to follow important instructions given by the management, material damage to machinery and equipment, unjustified and repeated absences) or (ii) an objective reason relating to the employer's need to reorganize its production activities or its labor force; however, in such cases, case law precedents state that the employer must seek, within its organization, another job for the employee in order to avoid the dismissal, if possible.

The dismissal must be ordered in writing and must indicate the reasons on which it is based. Moreover, whenever a dismissal is due to the employee's conduct (constituting either just cause or justified grounds, depending on the gravity), the employer must follow a specific disciplinary procedure set forth by the law, so that the employee is given the opportunity to defend his or her position before being dismissed.

Upon termination of their employment, employees are entitled to:

(a) The payment of a severance indemnity (the so-called *"TFR,"* which is accrued in the employer's financial statements during the term of employment and amounts to approximately to one month's salary for each year of seniority);

(b) The payment of some minor termination indemnities (payment in lieu of unused holidays and in lieu of unused paid leaves of absence, accrued prorata 13th month's salary, and so on); and

(c) A notice period, the duration of which varies according to the employees' seniority and professional level and is established in the applicable national labor collective agreement. In case the employer exempts the employees from working during the notice period, the employees must receive a corresponding payment in lieu of notice, which is equal to the normal salary (plus social security charges thereon) that would have been paid during the notice period. Payment under (a) and (b) is always due in case of dismissal, while the notice period payment outlined in (c) is not due in case of a dismissal for "just cause."

Any employee dismissed may bring a legal action if the employee deems that his or her dismissal was not properly justified. An action before the labor court must be preceded by an out-of-court challenge of the dismissal by means of any written document to employer (within 60 days of the dismissal) and by a mandatory attempt to reach a settlement before the local labor office. In the event that the absence of justified grounds is confirmed by the labor court, the consequences for the employer differ, according to whether that employer exceeds the "15-employee threshold."

The threshold is determined using the following criteria:

- If the employer is staffed with more than 15 employees per production unit (or more than 60 employees as a whole, even if split into production units which do not exceed the 15-employee threshold each), the employer will be required to reinstate the employee in his or her previous position and to pay him or her damages amounting to the salary accrued between the date of dismissal and the date of reinstatement (such indemnity must not be lower than five months' salary). Without prejudicing the right to this indemnity, the employee can elect to waive reinstatement and ask for the payment of an additional 15 months' salary.

- If the employer is staffed with fewer than 15 employees, the employer will be required to pay the employee an indemnity ranging between two-and-a-half and six months' salary. For the purposes of calculating such indemnity, reference has to be made to the so-called global salary of the employee (i.e., the annual base salary, including fringe benefits, divided by 12, plus the average of the bonuses paid the three years preceding the termination of employment, if any).

The strict compliance requirement along with indemnity payments required with a termination can lead an uninformed international partner to unintended lengthy and costly legal battle.

CHAPTER 3

Comparative Analysis of the U.S. Federal Worker Adjustment and Retraining Notification Act (WARN Act) and the Relevant Workforce Protection Laws in Germany and Italy

Germany and Italy are subject to directives and regulations of the European Union and to the decisions of the European Court of Justice and the European Court of Human Rights. European Court (EC), as a result of dealing with unemployment and seeing the need to address jobs security, issued a Council Directive of February 17, 1975 on the Approximation of the Laws of the Member States Relating to Collective Redundancies (layoffs) (the "Directive"). The Directive requires that when a company contemplates mass dismissal, the management must announce such a dismissal at least 30 days before initiating layoffs. This 30-day period attempts to provide labor the opportunity to participate in decision making and collaborate with management on feasibility of avoiding the dismissal. If the dismissal is deemed to be unavoidable, then labor and management will move on to discuss mitigating effects. This enhanced labor participation gives employees a voice and increases job security.

The WARN Act

In 1988, the U.S. Congress enacted legislation, WARN, to address mass layoffs. WARN requires that employers notify their employees and the local government prior to implementing the dismissals. "The most important difference between WARN and the European practice under the Directive is that WARN contemplates no role for employees or employee representatives in either determining the need for layoffs nor how to mitigate their impact on effected employees." WARN, contrary to the Directive, does not require negotiations between labor and management in addition to notice. WARN sets out the procedure that employers must follow prior to executing a mass dismissal or plant closing. "The objective seems, as much as anything else, to be designed to encourage some opportunity for public pressure to be organized against an employer contemplating layoffs." "The three substantive sections of WARN include its definitions and their scope, the required notice procedure, and the remedy to which affected employees are entitled."

WARN applies only to those businesses that employ 100 or more employees. Excluded from this threshold are temporary employees, defined as those who are either hired with the understanding that their employment is only for the duration of a particular project, or those who are hired to operate a temporary facility. Thus, the definition necessarily excludes seasonal workers as well. Also, outside the reach of WARN are employees out of work due to a strike or lock-out. Further, employees who are permanently replaced because of participation in an economic strike are not included in compiling the threshold.

Employers must dismiss a statutory number of the employees included in this threshold to have effectuated a "mass dismissal" under WARN. Like the Directive, WARN defines this statutory number in terms of the number of employees dismissed over a 30-day period in relation to the number of employees usually employed at a given site. To execute a mass dismissal, an employer must permanently dismiss at least 50 employees at one site. In the alternative, the employer must temporarily dismiss either 500 total or 33 percent of all employees.

Employers are, thus, not required to give notice at all unless the statutory minimum number of employees will experience an "employment loss." The term "employment loss" excludes many types of employees. Employees whose employers have offered them work at different sites, provided the new sites are within reasonable commuting distance, do not experience an employment loss under WARN. Also excluded are employees who accept such offers notwithstanding the fact that the new sites are not within a reasonable distance. Both of these exclusions are conditioned upon the fact that the transfer will not disrupt employment for more than six months.

Once employers have decided to dismiss a sufficient number of employees, the second substantive section of WARN comes into play. This section requires employers to notify their employees. Employers are also required to notify both the state-dislocated worker unit and local government of the pending dismissal at least 60 days prior to the execution of the plant closure or dismissal.

This notice period is somewhat flexible. Employers may reduce the notice period to "as much notice as is practicable" in three circumstances.

> Under the faltering company exception, employers who actively seek capital to avoid a closing or lay-off may shorten the period if they have a good faith belief that giving notice would frustrate their efforts. Employers may also reduce the notice period when confronted with unforeseen business circumstances at the time notice would normally have been required. Finally, employers need not give any notice if the mass dismissal or plant closing is due to a natural disaster and the giving of notice is impracticable.

Where the employer fails to give adequate notice, the third section of WARN provides a remedy for those employees who have been wrongfully discharged. In essence, employers are liable for back-pay for each day of the violation. In addition, employers are liable for the value of any benefits to which the employees were entitled while on the job. Employers must also pay a civil fine for failure to notify local officials.

Employers may mitigate their liability in four ways. First, they may pay the employees their wages during the period of the violation. Second, they may deduct from the initial calculation of 60 days wages, any voluntary and unconditional payments made to the employees. Third, they may deduct any payment made to a third party on behalf of the employee during the period of the violation. Fourth, they may mitigate their liability by demonstrating good faith beliefs that their actions would not violate WARN.

The courts have reviewed two of the exceptions that allow employers to reduce the notice period to "as much notice as is practicable." These are the exception for unforeseen business circumstances and the faltering company exception. With respect to the former, the court determined the scope of "unforeseeable," while for the latter, the court clarified the meaning of the phrase "actively seeking capital."

Under WARN, employers facing unforeseeable circumstances that adversely affect their businesses are excused from providing their employees with 60 days notice, but only if such notice would be impracticable or creates an undue hardship. Examples of such unforeseeable circumstances include natural disasters and sudden, dramatic changes in business conditions such as cost, price, or declines in customer orders. *In Jones v. Kayser-Roth Hosiery, Inc.,* the court held that the business judgment of the employer governs the determination of whether a business circumstance was reasonably unforeseeable. In determining whether the conduct of the employer was reasonable, the court compared the action taken by the employer with the action that a reasonably prudent employer in the same market would have taken. If the reasonably prudent employer would consider a given circumstance unforeseeable in light of the objective facts, then no notice is required. The same standard applies to determine how much notice is practical under the circumstances. Employers are also excused from providing the 60 days notice required by WARN if at the time the notice would have been required, they had been actively seeking capital or business that would have thwarted the need for a dismissal. In *Local 397 v. Midwest Fasteners, Inc.,* the court established a three-prong test for determining the validity of the invocation of the faltering company exception. Under this test, employers must first show the specific steps they have taken to obtain capital or new business. Employers must then show the basis for their good-faith belief that the notice would have prevented them from obtaining the needed capital. To satisfy the third prong of the court's test, employers must show that they notified the employees as soon as practicable, and explain why earlier notice was not given. The court concluded that negotiations for the sale of a business are not equivalent to "actively seeking capital." Thus, where the sale will result in a layoff or closure, notice must be given. Courts have also considered the remedial provisions of WARN.

WARN clearly states that its remedies are exclusive and attempts to expand them to include punitive damages have proven futile. In *Finnan v. L.F. Rothschild & Co.,* the court pointed out that Congress could have chosen to codify common law rules that permit punitive damages, but that it had chosen not to do so. The court concluded that Congress did not intend claimants to receive punitive damages.

Under WARN, the employer may avoid liability by claiming that they do not employ enough workers to fall under the scope of WARN. Judicial interpretations of WARN favor the employer and exempt part-time and temporary workers from being included in the requisite number to trigger WARN. Such judicial stance makes it more difficult for workers to compile sufficient numbers to trigger WARN.

Today, living in a reality of an economic downturn, many companies are shedding employees while not always complying with the notice required under the WARN. This is not just a current occurrence. On the 20th Anniversary of the WARN act, in a speech by Brown, Hon. Sherrod, a U.S. Senator from the State of Ohio, speaking at the hearing of the Committee on Health, Education, Labor, and Pensions, United States Senate, One Hundred Tenth Congress, second session, stated that "Most employers who are covered fail to comply with the law either out of ignorance or because the penalties and enforcement are so weak that they can, in fact, be ignored." At the same hearing Mr. Brown introduced legislation aimed at closing the loopholes and providing the tools necessary for enforcement of the rules.

In 2013, WARN act and its applicability and compliance continued to be a hot topic due to the ongoing economic challenges. Congressional Republicans criticized the Obama administration over what they say is a free pass being given to defense companies facing major layoffs from looming federal spending cuts. The Republicans objected the Labor Department advise to defense contractors that they would not need to observe the two-month layoff notification and the White House Office of Management and Budget went so far in support of that advise as to state it would reimburse companies that are sued by employees for breaking the law. Clearly, the WARN act continues to suffer from waivers and loopholes.

The European Directive

The European Court of Justice, on the other hand, has consistently interpreted the Directive in conformity with its policy objectives to protect the worker. The result of this construction demonstrates that the Court of Justice will not allow the Member States to derogate from the language of the Directive in fashioning their implementing legislation to assure worker protection. "The Directive has broader coverage and lower thresholds thus covering a much greater segment of the employee population than does the WARN."

The Directive consists of three substantive sections. The first section defines the terms and the scope of the Directive, while the second section establishes the procedure for consultation between management and labor, and notification of the government labor authority. When the management-labor consultations fail to avoid a collective redundancy, the last section of the Directive sets forth the method by which an employer may effectuate the dismissal. The Directive's first section defines a collective redundancy in terms of the number of employees dismissed in relation to the number of employees normally employed at a given site. The Directive allows each Member State to choose one of two thresholds. The first threshold operates over a 30-day period. Under this option, businesses that employ between 20 and 100 employees must dismiss at least ten employees to trigger the Directive. Those that maintain a workforce of 100–300 employees must dismiss at least 10 percent of the employees to trigger the Directive. Businesses that employ at least 300 workers trigger the Directive by dismissing at least 30 workers. The second, less stringent, option operates over a 90-day period. Under this option, businesses that dismiss 20 employees, regardless of the size of their labor force, trigger the Directive. In addition to setting up the two thresholds, the first section of the Directive excludes four classes of employees from its scope. First, the Directive excludes those employees hired to complete a specific contract and those hired specifically for a limited period. These employees, however, remain within the scope of the Directive if the dismissal occurs before the task is completed or before the limited period elapses. Second, the Directive excludes employees of public administrative bodies or establishments governed by public law. The third exclusion encompasses the crews of sea-going vessels. Fourth, the Directive excludes those employees who lose their jobs due to the closing of the business as the result of a judicial decision. Once the employer decides to dismiss a sufficient number of employees to trigger the Directive, the second section of the Directive requires the management and labor to embark on a detailed consultative process. Article 2 requires the employer to provide the representatives of the employees with all relevant information, such as the number of employees that will be dismissed, the number of workers normally employed, and the period over which the redundancies will be effected. The employer must also supply the representative of the employees with the reasons, in writing, for the redundancies. The reason for this transfer of information is to aid the representatives of the employees in making constructive proposals. In addition to providing this information, employers must simultaneously notify the government labor authority and meet with the representative of their employees. During the meeting, the labor and management discuss the possibility of avoiding the dismissal. If they determine that a dismissal is the only viable solution, they propose and discuss methods to minimize the effect of the dismissal on workers. The discussion at the meeting may also involve alternatives to dismissal, such as salary freezes or pay cuts, uncompensated overtime, a reduction in work hours, workforce attrition, or temporary layoffs with priority rehiring. Where the management and labor determine that a collective redundancy is the only viable alternative, the third section of the Directive dictates the method by which employers must effectuate the dismissal. The employers must first submit a detailed written report to the public employment authority.

Upon receiving the report, the public employment authority has 30 days to evaluate the severity of the dismissal and to prepare the community for the sudden flood of unemployed. While waiting for this 30-day period to expire, employers may not dismiss any employees. The 30-day notice period is somewhat flexible. In some circumstances, the Member States may permit the public employment authority to lengthen the period. In these cases, the public employment authority may extend the period to a maximum of 60 days. The provisions of the Directive represent the minimum standards required by the EC. In implementing the Directive, the Member States are free to impose standards that are more severe than those required by the Directive. Many of the Member States have done so by lowering the threshold numbers or strengthening the notice requirements. The overall effect has been a level of workplace rights enhanced beyond that envisioned by the EC. The Directive contains one significant loophole that has emerged over the past few years as a result of increased international corporate restructuring. The Directive does not provide for the situation where the decision to effectuate a redundancy is made by a controlling parent company or head office, as opposed to the employing subsidiary or branch. In such a circumstance, the immediate employer may not have access to all of the information that it is required to pass on to the employees' representatives and the government labor authority. In order to fill this gap, the Commission has proposed an amendment to the Directive. This amendment will require that the procedures of the Directive apply regardless of where the decision to dismiss was made. The remedy, as provided by the amendment, for failure to fulfill the notification and consultation procedure is the nullity of the collective redundancy.

German Labor Law Framework

The German constitution was adopted on May 23, 1949, and is referred to as the Basic Law. With its amendment by the Unification Treaty of August 31, 1990, and the Federal Statute of September 23, 1990, the Basic Law has become the Constitution of the unified West and East Germany (former Federal Republic of Germany and German Democratic Republic). The Basic Law guarantees freedom of association as well as free choice of occupation and prohibition of forced labor. It also establishes the principle of equal treatment, and in particular, obliges the state to support the effective realization of gender equality. The major sources of labor law are federal legislation, collective agreements, works agreements, and case law. There is not one consolidated labor code; minimum labor standards are laid down in separate acts on various labor related issues, which are supplemented by the government's ordinances.

Because most German companies are "unionized," the different unions concentrate negotiating individual terms that are much better and more employee-favorable than the basic labor law. Unions even go so far as to negotiate different terms for different regions and districts depending on the cost of living of such region and the demographics of the employee group.

Labor legislation is interpreted by labor courts. Some matters, especially strike regulation, are partly or even totally left to case law. Collective agreements (Tarifverträge) are legally binding as long as they keep in line with the statutory minimum standards. They are usually concluded at the branch level by the appropriate trade union and employers' association, and hence cover one branch (or parts of it) and either a region or the entire country. However, sometimes, collective bargaining also takes place at the enterprise level. In 1999, 8 percent of the employees in Western Germany and 11 percent of those in Eastern Germany fell under an enterprise-based collective agreement. Collective agreements are always binding for members of the relevant trade union and employers' association. Provided certain conditions are met, the binding power can be extended to all employees of the branch in the respective region. In 1999, 65 percent of the employees in Western Germany and 46 percent of those in Eastern Germany were covered by a branch-level collective agreement. In practice, the *establishment* (Betrieb) also plays an important role. The establishment is the organizational unit where particular working objectives are pursued. At this level, conditions of work such as those determined in the Works Constitution Act may be, or in certain cases, must be laid down in *works agreements* (Betriebsvereinbarung). These are written agreements concluded between the employer and the works council (a body representing the employees of the establishment).

Workers' representation in the enterprise is governed by the Works Constitution Act. This act is decisively based on the term *establishment.* In an establishment regularly employing five or more employees, its employees may decide to elect a works council, of which the period of office is four years. In practice, works councils are set up especially in medium size and big enterprises, and much more rarely in small enterprises: In 1999, works councils were organized in 97.5 percent of establishments employing more than 1,000 workers, but only in 4.2 percent of establishments employing from 5 to 20 employees.

The number of members of a works council is determined by the number of workers normally employed in the establishment. It varies from 1 member in establishments occupying from 5 to 20 workers to 31 members in establishments occupying from 7,001 to 9,000 employees. In establishments with more than 9,000 workers, the number of members of a works council is increased by 2 members for every additional 3,000 workers. Manual and nonmanual workers have separate representation on a works council.

The works council has rights of participation as well as of codetermination. The right of participation includes the right to be informed and to make recommendations. The right of codetermination is by far of much more practical consequence, because it entails the possibility of blocking a decision of the employer, which is dependent on the works council's agreement. It covers subjects such as work rules, working time including overtime and holiday roster, methods of pay, the introduction and use of technical devices for monitoring employees' conduct and performance, accident prevention and health protection, fringe benefits, and the provision and withdrawal of company-owned housing. However, wages must never be determined at the establishment level.

The works council and the employer agree within the limits of an applying collective agreement, often by concluding a written works agreement. They must cooperate on the basis of mutual trust. Any dispute must be settled by legal proceedings either leading to a court order or resulting in a decision of a conciliation committee. The conciliation committee is set up in case of disagreements in matters of codetermination. It is composed of an independent chairperson and an equal number of employer's and employees' representatives.

Another essential duty of the works council and the employer is to supervise the equal treatment of all employees in the establishment. This includes the prohibition against discrimination against the works council members, who are furthermore safeguarded against dismissal by special provisions. Workers' representation may also exist at the *enterprise* level via a central works council that deals with enterprise-related matters. Its setting up is mandatory if the enterprise has several establishments with the existing works councils. This body is composed of representatives of manual and nonmanual workers who are sent by the affected works councils. Its period of office is unlimited.

Provided that legally independent enterprises are merged into a combine, even a combine works council may be created, in so far as the central
works councils decide to have one. In a number of companies that operate branch establishments or subsidiaries in various EC Member States,
special "works councils" have been set up for the purpose of voicing the
interests of employees in all their establishments throughout the community. These bodies do not, however, have institutional backing comparable
to that of the German-style works council, nor corresponding rights.

Italian Labor Law Framework

The Italian Constitution was approved by the Parliament in December
1947 and came into effect on January 1, 1948. The Country is organized
as a centralized state, divided into regions, provinces, and municipali-
ties. Sicily, Sardinia, Alto Adige (German-speaking region), Valle d'Aosta
(French-speaking region), and Friuli (a region with Slavic minorities)
have special statutes. Article 39 of the Italian Constitution guarantees
freedom to organize, join a trade union, and engage in trade union activity in the workplace. Trade union density in Italy is above the EU's 27
percent average, according to the administrative data of the three trade
union confederations. In 2010, 36.5 percent of the Italian employees
were members of a trade union (retired employees excluded; in 1995, net
trade union density was 38.1 percent).

The unions joining the biggest federations have a very important
function in collective bargaining in public employment and receive protection in view of trade union activity at the plant level. The Workers'
Statute, 1970, regulates plant-level union activity. The Statute has been
an important means of support of the unions at plant level. The Workers'
Statute of 1970 gives the workers the right to organize a plant-level union
representation structure (Rappresentanza sindacale aziendale, RSA). The
tripartite agreement of July 1993 introduced—in addition to the RSA—a
so-called unitary workplace union structure (Rappresentanza sindacale
unitaria, RSU). This body is elected by all employees, but representatives
are usually elected through trade union lists. Therefore, it includes features of both works councils (the broad active electorate) and trade union

bodies (the almost exclusive inclusion of trade union representatives). The establishment of RSUs confirms the traditional system of single-channel representation in Italy, whereby union and employee representation are entrusted to a single body, as opposed to dual-channel systems where union delegates operate alongside works councils.

Two-thirds of the representatives in the RSU are elected by the workforce (both union and nonunion members); one-third of the positions are reserved for the trade union organizations affiliated to the signatory organizations of the sectoral national collective agreement (Contratto Collettivo Nazionale di Lavoro, CCNL) applied in the company. RSUs, when present, have all of the rights attributed to RSAs by law or collective agreements (1970 Workers' Statute rights, as well as rights regarding information and consultation). Since 1993, RSUs have been able to negotiate at plant level on issues that are delegated from the industry-wide level. RSUs have tended to replace RSAs, which are now usually found only in very small companies.

In researching this paper, I consulted with Elena Ghigo of Johnson and Johnson, Italy, who summarized the acquisition process in clear and concise terms: "In Italy, when an acquisition occurs (i.e., a company absorbs another or part of Italian Company), Italian law provides that all the absorbed employees are transferred to the new/acquiring company maintaining their previous contracts with all relevant benefits and they also maintain seniority. In this case, the passage from one company to the other is automatic and the consent of the employee is not required. So, the employment relationship continues seamlessly, and the employee maintains all rights accrued up to the date of the transfer. In order to be able to renegotiate the previous contract, the new/acquiring company has to achieve the consent of the employee."

> In case of redundancies, Italian law prescribes that three aspects must be taken into consideration when operating toward redundancy and they have to be taken into account when identifying the workers which will be dismissed. The above mentioned aspects are: technical and organizational requirements of the company, seniority and family burdens of the employee. If a company employs more than 15 people and is contemplating to dismiss

more than 5 employees in a 120 days period, it is forced to draw upon redundancy and not simple summon dismissals due to economical issues. The collective dismissal implies a particular procedure that combines labor union participation, governmental authorities and the company in a dialogue that, through various steps, strives to reach a shared solution.

CHAPTER 4

"Soft Due Diligence" Investigation Relating to Family and Medical Leave

In summarizing some of the different segments to consider for a soft due diligence investigation, we must compare the social systems, legislation, and customs of family leave plans in the United States, Germany, and Italy.

The diagnostics to support a "soft due diligence" analysis and insure a precise and strategic focus will require an investigative team that far surpasses the group of investors, financiers, bankers, accountants, and lawyers usually assembled during the preacquisition phase.

Further support of "soft due diligence" is that the EU countries have begun to demonstrate an ability to exercise economic and political power as a bloc, often in a manner that is different than what is exercised in the United States. In 2001, the EU rejected General Electric's bid to purchase Honeywell, a bid that was initially approved by U.S. authorities. The Commission was of the view that the merger would not increase efficiency, rather, it would strengthen the market dominance of GE-hurt competition and customers. This was a significant and unexpected blow to General Electric, and the merger with Honeywell subsequently fell apart. The EU has also taken the initiative in opposing the U.S. tariffs on imported steel and appears willing to continue to litigate antitrust issues against Microsoft, despite the settlement between Microsoft and the U.S. government.

These examples illustrate that the progress the EU has made in economic integration is providing a base from which the bloc can exercise economic power to offset the United States and to protect the interests of the EU. As labor standards define the work environment, shape the conditions of employment, and have implications for trade, foreign direct investment, employment, and economic competitiveness, it is critical that "soft due diligence" be an integral part of the preacquisition research.

Another theory why American investors do not include a soft due diligence approach is the bill for this variety of *due diligence* could come to millions in terms of fees, without any guarantees that the acquisition will be successful. To include other professionals requires a substantial investment, one which would make the difference of success or failure, but one costly aspect that most investors would just as soon skip. (Kind of like Scarlett's attitude in *Gone with the Wind*, "I can't think about that right now. I will deal with it tomorrow.")

Much of the present business literature supports the skeptical or pessimistic track record of merged or acquired companies. Studies show that many—if not most—mergers are doomed to fail. Why? Sometimes, as with MCI WorldCom and Sprint, they fall apart due to regulatory pressure before they ever take place. Sometimes, as with Quaker and Snapple, it is because one company overestimated the worth of the other and overpaid. Sometimes, as with Kmart and Sears, it is simply poor product, market, or resource synergy. Sometimes, because companies forget there are human beings working in this integration.

When mergers come up, these are the causes often discussed. But *culture*, in part because it is so difficult to measure or manage, is all-too-often overlooked.

Yet, according to the Society for Human Resource Management (SHRM), over 30 percent of mergers fail because of simple culture incompatibility.

Not every factor of a merger is going to be within your control, but the more time spent on the culture you are planning on moving into, the more likely the transition will be successful. It is the onus of the lawyer to convince the American investors they represent to adjust their perspectives to fit the legal, synergized cultural, and social realities that prevail in Europe [specifically for this book, Germany and Italy] with respect to family and medical leave issues and, indeed, the entire relationship between work-life and home-life. Perhaps, the greatest challenge facing top managers during the transition from two organizations to one integrated organization is establishing a process, and decisions have to be made to reconcile such differences, so that the synergies planned for can be achieved.

Defining Mergers and Acquisitions and the Lawyers' Responsibility

Mergers and acquisitions (M&As) are increasing with competitive and financial pressures of globalization. Through M&As, firms seek strategic positioning, industrywide consolidation, increased market share and shareholder value, synergy through economies of scale revenue enhancement, risk reduction, shared cost of product development, and improved access to markets and new technologies.

A merger is the joining or integration of two previously discrete entities. It occurs when two companies integrate to form a new company with shared resources and corporate objectives. An acquisition occurs when an organization acquires sufficient shares to gain control or ownership of another organization. Other positive organizational effects include acquiring new capabilities and resources, cutting costs, and defending against a (hostile) take over.

The lawyer assigned to evaluate an M&A has an obligation to distinguish between "hard" and "soft" human resource (HR) practices during the beginning phases of the merger or acquisition. The first phase usually includes pay differentials between the two organizations, trade union policy and density, differences in employment benefits such as pension funds, level of in-company training commitment, and possible retrenchments; taking into consideration that during the soft due diligence investigation, the lawyer must keep in mind that not all deals are good. John Chambers, CEO Cisco Systems stated in 1998:

> We've killed nearly as many acquisitions as we've made...even when they are very tempting. I believe it takes courage to walk away from a deal. It really does. You can get caught up in winning the acquisition and lose sight of what will make it successful. That's why we take such a disciplined approach.

Identifying Risks

Risk is what business expansion is about! But, risk can be substantially reduced by integrating and redefining the target culture with the corporate values of the new company. When you start the M&A investigation procedure, you will need to identify the differences between your company [U.S.] values, procedures, laws, and policies with the new company's policies, laws, and procedures governing family leave plans. The following sample list identifies critical areas for consideration: (1) social ideology of the country, including the history and the present status of the country's political, economic, and social values and the systems in place to implement them, (2) the purposes of the legislation, and (3) the coverage of the law. These are often practically interrelated, but reflect different theoretical perceptions. Not to mention discovering a way to integrate and combine values, which are not easily joined.

One of the best illustrations for including soft due diligence is to look at Jack Welch, CEO, who led the ever powerful General Electric (now run by Jeff Emmelt) to create the acquisition fever for which GE is renowned. In the GE empire, very few days go past without purchasing, merging, or divesting one of its businesses. GE has a powerful set of processes in place to undertake both soft due diligence and postacquisition integration. They commit to them every time. The same performance is mirrored by Fred Goodwin, CEO of Royal Bank of Scotland. In his hands, the business has grown to become the sixth biggest bank in the world. The reputation of these two companies would allow one to conclude that their business models are well-tested and more than likely contain a series of soft due diligence procedures and strategies that can be utilized for different size businesses, in different locals with different geographical cultures.

Another illustration is how the different countries define maternity leave, which usually refers to leave, which addresses the physical demands placed on pregnant women and new biological mothers. Most of the industrial countries prescribe at least 15 weeks including father's leave, but the U.S. definition of maternity leave is much narrower in that it is strictly limited to pregnancy and childbirth with a six-week recovery period, with the leave restricted to the mother and no possibility of extensions. But, the biggest difference between Germany's laws and the FMLA is that Germany provides generous cash maternity benefits including any extensions.

Creating the Right Culture

So, how can you create a culture that will help ensure the success of your M&A—develop a strategy? Without a strategy that includes "soft" due diligence supporting a successful cultural and systemic integration, the lawyer will not be able to evaluate whether there are salient differences in employee benefits between the target country and the United States or whether they can be reconciled to permit the M&A to optimize the cost-benefit balance. Premerger planning has a direct impact on the businesses post-merger cultural and community integration. The lawyer cannot assume that a change may occur through the efflux of time.

CHAPTER 5

Family Leave Practices

Comparison of Maternity, Paternity, and Family Leave Laws of Target Countries and the United States

The following chapter explores in more detail some of the issues for the failure of mergers and acquisitions (M&As) by an American investor in the EU. Recent years have seen a huge growth in the European M&A, and considerable attention has been given to how these deals arise and are completed. Throughout the readings, it has been increasingly recognized that success of a business performance cannot be separated from national or regional cultural influences.

One scheme as to why American business considering European acquisitions have failed is generally owing to the mentality of U.S. employers toward our own Family and Medical Leave Act of 1993 (FMLA)—an attitude that has affected the weight of importance of an American investor, his or her team, and amount of time CEOs will give to researching other countries customs and laws during the preacquisition research stage for a potential M&A to uncover "hidden costs."

In general, the U.S. employment model is based on the primacy of market forces. The basic view in the United States is that optimal labor market outcomes are those that are produced by the functioning of the market; therefore, government regulation, and to some extent, the scope of collective bargaining should be minimized. The EU, on the other hand, bases its conception of employment on the principle that unregulated markets create an imbalance of power between the employer and employee; therefore, government regulation and institutionalized unions are necessary to create countervailing power in the labor market that protects employees.

Europe has created a capitalist system based on private property but with a highly regulated labor market, creating a wide range of employee rights embodied in overarching governing regulation. The United States, on the other hand, has created a capitalist system based on private property and lightly regulated labor markets, with relatively few rights guaranteed to employees.

Because each company believes its way of operating is how god intended life to be, major differences in culture could be difficult to face. An important policy question to be examined is how much of any differences in the economic performance of the two systems can be attributed to labor market regulation and protections.

Employee Benefit Costs

Benefits cover a wide scope of areas: time off, maternity leave, health and life insurance, and pensions, and what appears to be a good plan for one country may not apply at all or may be well-below the statutory minimum requirements in another country.

One theory for the difference in social benefits policy is that, unlike the United States, the majority of European countries are considered to be social states. Another theory is that there has not been a war fought within the United States' borders since the Civil War, whereas in Europe, almost every country suffered major devastation from both World Wars. Policies may differ because of the conflicting goals of the feminist movements in the United States and in Europe, and finally, the laws that govern family leave. Whereas in the United States, the feminist movement focused on gaining equal treatment for men and women, in Europe, the movement focused on gaining special treatment for mothers.

"EU is a federal concept and EU law of employment is just emerging." Thus, the varying forms of compliance by Member States make it difficult for multinational employers to establish a uniform policy across European Union Member States, as each state's provisions are somewhat different. While the Directive is in and of itself a binding regulation for Member States, it has the limitation of being just a framework under which Member States may create their own regulatory structure, making uniformity nearly impossible. Though the disparities in the United States and European Union law on family leave make compliance difficult on multinationals, neither the law of the European Union nor the United

States has been hesitant to sanction violators of international law in the past. While multinational corporations face the threshold threat of disciplinary action by the Court of Justice of the European Communities, their worries cannot stop there. In addition, multinationals must deal with the worker participation law concept ever-present in European Union nations. In a sense, such worker-participation laws function much like the U.S. concept of a labor union, in that employee groups are set up to discuss relevant issues, such as working conditions and wages. These participation groups go far beyond standing up for workers' rights; however, "…[t]he European worker groups are run in cooperation with management. In the United States, unions are not really trying to manage the company…." Thus, violation of the Directive by multinationals will mean loss of goodwill of the corporations' employees and of the surrounding community; in addition, such violations will also cause a loss of support by such worker participation groups, a key body in the European labor force itself. Therefore, the stakes of noncompliance for multinational corporations are high.

CHAPTER 6

Target Country—Germany— Family Leave Benefits

Mandatory Maternity Leave

Germany's recovery from an unemployment disease, birth rate decline since WWII, and its resilience to the Great Recession is remarkable. Its success story makes it a showcase for labor policy and labor market reforms. Flexible management of working time (through overtime and short-time work, time accounts, and labor hoarding), social cohesion, and controlled unit labor costs, combined with a rigid, incentive-oriented labor policy supported by effective program evaluation, define the characteristics of a strong reference model. As early as 1878, Germany inaugurated the first Maternity Leave Act. The legislated protections provided three weeks of leave after birth and coverage and benefits continue to increase.

"GroKo" is the new buzzword in German politics. It stands for "GroßeKoalition" or Grand Coalition, the new German government composed of the Christian Democratic Union (CDU) and the left-wing Social Democratic Party (SPD) who got together and formed the "Coalition Treaty." One (of many) employment law project proposed in the Coalition Treaty is to enable parents or relatives to return to full-time work after "family-related" part time work. The new government wants to implement this legal entitlement by 2014 for any kind of family-related situation. For example: if an employee wants to take care of his or her older children for a year or organize permanent care for his or her aging parent, those employees shall be allowed to reduce their working time for a certain period and then resume their full-time job.

Motherhood is made a little easier if you happen to be an employed woman working for a German company. You will actually be provided paid mandatory time-off from work, before and after childbirth. This is revelatory news for many English-speaking expats. Basically, the

Mutterschutzgesetz, Maternity Protection Act of 1968, was instituted to ensure that expecting mothers are not discriminated against when applying for jobs and to provide them with added protection from being dismissed from work as a result of their pregnancy or arrival of their newborn child. This law actually goes well beyond that fundamental claim and provides much more.

The European Union had "further to go" in improving its rights for pregnant women and parents in general, because blatant discrimination against these classes has been allowed in the past, unlike in the United States.

Under the Maternity Protection Statute (*Mutterschutzgesetz* or *MuSchG*), revised on June 20, 2002, expectant mothers must not be employed for a period of six weeks before the date of expected childbirth and for a period of eight weeks after giving birth (12 weeks in the case of pre-term or multiple births), hereinafter "maternity leave." This Act ensures expecting mothers that are deemed unable to work are not financially penalized during the *Schutzfrist*. The Maternity Protection Pay is issued by the employer and must be at least the same amount of a 13-week wages average or of the last three months before pregnancy.

The United States is the only industrial developed nation without paid maternity leave. In fact, it's one of the only countries without any paid leave. Although workers are eligible for 12 weeks of parental leave, thanks to the Family and Medical Leave Act of 1993, the leave is unpaid and workers are only eligible if they are employed by a big company or a government agency. A 2009 report by the Congressional Research Service found that just 8 percent of the private sector employees are offered parental leave.

In Germany, even before maternity leave begins, there are specific compulsory prohibitions against difficult physical work; work that exposes the mother to damaging emissions of dangerous substances or rays; dust, gases, or vapors; heat, cold, or humidity; or vibrations or noise; and against other, more specific categories of work. In addition, expectant mothers must not be employed to the extent that, according to a doctor's certificate, the mother's or the child's life or health would be put at risk if employment were continued.

During maternity leave, women who are members of a statutory health insurance provider receive maternity pay from their health insurance provider; other women, not covered, their paid leave is calculated in the same way as if the woman was covered by statutory health insurance plan. Women usually receive a maximum of €13 per day (U.S. $17.31), up to a maximum of €210 in total, during maternity leave from the government. The employer is then required to pay the difference between the applicable maternity pay and the woman's average salary or wages net of tax and social security contributions, calculated on the basis of the wage statements for the last three months or 13 weeks before the commencement of maternity leave.

Termination within the probationary period, during which the protections of the Termination Protection Statute do not apply, is not permissible in the case of a pregnant woman and their job is protected for a three-year period. Only in particular cases where the termination is unrelated to the woman's condition during pregnancy or the four months' period following childbirth, for example, in the event of a plant closing, the authorities may declare a termination permissible upon the employer's application.

Like the FMLA, before a woman can take advantage of the termination protection for mothers, the employer must be informed of the employee's pregnancy or that she has given birth. At the latest, the woman must inform the employer within two weeks after receiving a notice of termination. Noncompliance with this deadline is disregarded if the woman is not responsible for it and if the failure to provide such information is made up without undue delay. The woman, on the other hand, may terminate her employment at any time during pregnancy or postchildbirth maternity leave with effect from the end of maternity leave.

Parental leave is a two-year, income-tested leave. Parents are also granted a three-year job-protected leave following childbirth. (This pertains only to parents whose employers have more than 15 employees.) Parents can split this leave or take it at the same time. Although both parents are eligible for this leave, less than 1 percent of the eligible fathers actually take this leave in Germany. An amendment to the comprehensive Federal Child Care Benefit Act (FCCBA) that went into effect in January 1986 made German benefits available to mothers (in the paid labor force or not) and to fathers (though reports show only 1.3 percent of the claims to be those of eligible men). Traditionally, social expectations have been that women will take on most, if not all, child care responsibilities. This traditional view has been reinforced by the reality that mothers tend to earn less at paid work than fathers do. Women's traditional gender roles and their disadvantage relative to men in the labor market work together to shift the responsibility of care for infants and young children heavily toward mothers.

Here are some condensed highlights from the Maternity Protection Act: Employers have to provide a healthy and safe work environment for expecting and nursing mothers; employers have to provide an adequate break room that can accommodate a reclining chair for expecting and nursing mothers who require it for their wellbeing; pregnant or nursing mothers are not banned from working in front of PC monitors, although it is popularly thought that magnetic fields are a health hazard—this claim has yet to be properly substantiated. However, employers are encouraged to create a diverse work routine so as to not overstress an expecting or nursing mother. The company doctor should be called upon to provide professional, medical input; expecting mothers are not permitted to perform heavy, physical labor or to work with or among materials, substances, and gases or in extreme elements that could be deemed potentially hazardous to their health; expecting and nursing mothers should not be exposed to compressed air, or radioactive material—chemical and biological pollutants could also be considered harmful; unemployment benefits while getting the child-rearing allowance.

In many cases, women can tack a period of up to three years of parental leave onto maternity leave. The legal bases for this are found in Sections 15 and 16 of the Federal Parental Pay and Leave Statute. If a mother or father wishes to avail her or himself of parental leave, she or he must apply to the employer in writing at least seven weeks before the leave is to commence. In that application, the employee must state for which periods until the child's second birthday she or he wishes to take parental leave. Parental leave can be taken in one or two parts; any further split requires the employer's consent.

In principle, extended parental leave can be taken only until the child's third birthday, but with the employer's consent, up to 12 months thereof can be taken until the child's eighth birthday. Parental leave may be taken, in full or in part, by each parent alone or jointly by both parents.

What Can an Employer Expect to Pay?

Parents are entitled to government benefits during at least part of their parental leave. For children born or adopted after December 31, 2006, parental pay amounts to 67 percent of the average pay received during the 12-month period preceding childbirth, with a minimum of €300 per month and a cap of €1,800 per month. Parental pay is provided for a maximum period of 12 months (under certain conditions 14 months).

Furthermore, during parental leave, each parent is entitled to request a reduction in working hours if the following circumstances exist: The employer has more than 15 employees on a regular basis (not including apprentices); the employment relationship has existed for more than six months without any interruption; working hours will be reduced for at least a two-month period to between 15 to 30 hours a week; the reduction in working hours does not conflict with urgent operational requirements; and the request for reduction is made in writing no less than seven weeks prior to the planned reduction.

Such request can be made only twice during parental leave. If the employer wishes to deny the requested reduction in working hours, it must do so in writing within four weeks, setting forth the reasons for denial. If the employer fails to grant the request, or does not grant the request in a timely manner, the employee may institute legal proceedings in the labor courts. The term Union has a very different connotation in the United States as compared with other countries. In most European countries, the employer will be working with either Works Councils or Trade Unions. The Unions, unlike in the United States, are mandated by statute in most cases and play a major role in work determination, training, wage rates, and redundancies, regulated by Work Councils.

For the employer to facilitate the part-time work request, the employer must organize substitutes or otherwise cover the shortfall in working time. If the employee shall be entitled to return to full-time again, the employers will need predictability (announcement requirements sufficiently in advance) and laws enabling him or her to hire substitutes temporarily. Otherwise, he will have too many employees on board when the part-time employee returns to full-time.

Women are well-protected in Germany from loss of employment due to dismissal from the beginning of pregnancy until four months following childbirth (*Schutzfrist*) through a *Kündigungsverbot*, Dismissal Ban. Only in extremely rare exceptions are employers permitted to dismiss a pregnant employee during this time.

If employer receives a Certificate of Expected Date of Delivery within two weeks of canceling a pregnant employees contract—the dismissal is usually retracted or nullified. Not many companies want to invest in the complicated and often unsuccessful undertaking of challenging the higher authorities on this subject.

Having the work done by coworkers—to facilitate the part-time work request—currently requires the employer to organize substitutes or otherwise cover the shortfall in working time. Heavier workloads for coworkers may, in the long run, lead to dissatisfaction and increased fluctuation, more error-prone work, and lower productivity. Hence, we would expect the costs of work-sharing solutions borne by the employer to be a function of the duration of leave such that employer costs will generally increase with increasing maternity leave duration.

If the employee shall be entitled to return to full-time again, the employers will need predictability (announcement requirements sufficiently in advance) and laws enabling him or her to hire substitutes temporarily. Otherwise, he or she will have too many employees on board when the part-time employee returns to full-time. It would be desirable (and can be expected) that the new laws will follow the pattern of the regulations on parental leave where such claim already exists. If the new model, once implemented, is widely used, this will mean an increasing administrative burden for employers, who once more will be encumbered with sociopolitical objectives of politics. The additional paid leave to care for family members will mean costs for the employers.

Existing studies on the effect of maternity leave provisions on women's labor market position concentrate on the duration of maternity leave as a proxy for the costs accruing to employers—the underlying hypothesis being that the longer the leave duration, the more human capital is being lost. In many cases, however, the loss of human capital during a limited absence of several months may not be the main cost factor for employers faced with a mother on leave who wishes to return to her previous job.

Moreover, it may well be the reorganization of work during absence and thereafter that causes a problem to the employer.

The United States maternity leave is unpaid, while mothers on maternity leave in Germany receive pay reaches up to a 100 percent of the wage—40 percent of these costs are borne by the employer. These costs of having to cofinance maternity pay add to the costs of reorganization.

CHAPTER 7

Target Country—Italy— Family Leave Benefits

Mandatory Leave

In Italy, parental leave is regulated mainly by the law (currently laws 1204 of 1971 and 903 of 1977). According to a law adopted in 1971 and amended many times since, pregnant women here are obligated to take off the last two months of pregnancy and the first three months following the birth—for a total of five months during which they receive full salary, 80 percent of it paid by the state. Having babies is a serious business everywhere. But, in Italy, working women are given the time to treat it almost like a job. Long paid leaves combined with free medical care are considered part of an Italian mother's birthright—one element of the safety net that middle-class taxpayers across Europe have both enjoyed and supported with very steep taxes for many decades now, in contrast to their middle-class counterparts in America, who by and large see social spending as money only for the poor.

The Italian Constitution, under Article 37, states that working women and men have equal rights as to salary and all protections of applicable laws. Moreover, it provides that a working woman must be granted work conditions that: (i) give her the opportunity to carry out her essential role within the family and (ii) ensure a special and adequate protection to the mother and the child.

After some delay, the 1996 EU Directive on parental leave has now been converted into Italian law. The aim of the new law is to enable a more satisfactory balance to be struck between family and work commitments. Accordingly, its innovative aspects are the extension of the duration of leave and the introduction of incentives designed to encourage the use of leave entitlement by fathers. Law no. 1204 of December 30, 1971, on this subject has been recently amended by Law no. 53 of March 8, 2000; Legislative Decree no. 151 of March 26, 2001, sets out the main principles relating to maternity rights: 1) a pregnant employee has the right to time off during working hours for medical appointments. Requests for such leave are not to be unreasonably refused; 2) a woman is entitled to maternity leave and salary during the following time periods: (i) a mandatory period of two months before the expected date of delivery, (ii) the days between the predicted date of delivery and actual date of delivery, (iii) a further mandatory period of three months after the delivery, (iv) an optional period of six months (during which the employee is paid at a reduced rate) until the child is eight years old), and (v) If there is only one parent, for a maximum of ten days a working mother is entitled to two hours paid leave a day (reduced to one hour if her working hours are less than six), until the child is one year old, in order to feed the baby.

The salary paid to the employee for the aforementioned periods is recoverable by the employer from the social security authorities (Istituto Nazionale di Previdenza Social [INPS]) as follows: (a) for 80 percent of the employee's salary for the mandatory periods and (b) for 30 percent of the employee's salary for the optional period for a maximum of six months until the child is three years old.

Optional Leave

In addition to the mandatory maternity leave governed by the laws, there are also benefits that are not written in legislation, but simply sanctioned by tradition. For instance, women with risky pregnancies are entitled, with the appropriate doctor's certificate, to take all nine months of pregnancy off. Likewise, mothers suffering from depression or mothers whose babies require special care can get other doctors' certificates, entitling them to stay away from work for up to three years. (In these cases, salaries are not automatically guaranteed.)

A pregnant employee cannot be dismissed during the pregnancy period and within the first year after birth of the child, except for just cause.

As a consequence of (i) several Italian Constitutional Court (Corte Costituzionale), judgments aimed at giving both parents the opportunity to take leave in order to look after their children and (ii) EU Directive 96/34/ECC, the Italian Parliament passed Law no. 53 of March 8, 2000, and Legislative Decree no. 151 of March 26, 2001, amending the previous legislation regarding parental leave.

Paternal Leave

The most significant amendments introduced by the Law no. 53 are the following: 1) the father is now entitled to take leave during the mandatory period of three months described under (iii) previously in case of mother's death or illness, or in the event that he has custody of the child, 2) both parents have the opportunity to take leave to care for their children during the optional period of six months described under (iv) earlier, 3) both parents are now entitled to two hours paid leave a day described under (v) previously, and 4) both parents independently are permitted to take leave (being paid at a reduced rate) in the event of their child's sickness until the child is eight years old, upon presentation of a medical certificate. Leave may be taken without any time limitations for illnesses of children from birth to three years old, and for not more than five working days per parent for children who are from three to eight years old.

In this respect, Law no. 104 of February 24, 2006, extended the same rights already granted to nonmanagerial employees to managers (dirigenti), which means that, since April 1, 2006, the salary paid to dirigenti during the aforementioned periods is recoverable by INPS, whereas before it was completely borne by the employer.

What Can an Employer Expect to Pay?

The law distinguishes between the purpose of the paid family leave under the following conditions: 1) recovering from a serious illness; 2) taking care of a seriously ill family member; and 3) caring for a newborn or newly adopted child.

In the first case, usually, the employer is bound for the payment of the income but, only for particular illnesses, INPS—Istituto Nazionale Previdenza Sociale (i.e., Social Security Service) provides relevant coverage after the fourth day of absence from work and the latter grants the payment of an allowance and the employer can only be demanded, if provided by specific provisions of the National CBA, to pay an integration of income paid by the Social Security Service. Therefore, for these particular categories, a percentage is paid by INPS and a percentage is paid by the employer. Normally, it is the employer who grants the payment of the total income on a regular basis, up to the maximum amount of time which is different for each category and provided for by the single National Collective Bargain Agreements. On the contrary, the allowance paid by the INPS after the fourth day is normally equal to 50 percent of the average daily wage from the fourth day to the 21st day of sickness and 66 percent of the average daily wage from the 21st day to the 180th day of sickness (exceptions are regulated within the single National Collective Bargain Agreements). Particular provisions of National Collective Bargain Agreements demand the employer to pay a further amount in order to grant the employees their full income.

In the second case, the employee is granted with three paid days of leave (per year) in case of death or serious illness of the spouse, a family member or of a relative within the second degree, and the income, in this case, is paid by the employer. In particular circumstances, the employee can ask to be acknowledged an extraordinary leave in case of serious and proved family-related issues. The leave can last maximum two years during the whole employment relationship. During the extraordinary leave, the normal salary is interrupted and the employee can be granted an allowance, which is normally anticipated by the employer, but refunded by the INPS. Paid family leave taken for the purpose of taking care of a seriously ill family member, the three days of paid leave are granted by the employer with no reductions. On the contrary, in case of extraordinary leave, only the Social Security Service grants a one-time allowance; therefore, the income is interrupted, but the employee maintains his job position.

In the third case, the mother (or the father if the mother is incapable of taking care of the child) of a newborn child or a newly adopted one can benefit of a paid leave and the income is usually paid in advance by the employer, which will be refunded by the INPS or paid directly by the latter if particular circumstances occur (e.g., when the employer is unable to fulfill the advanced financial obligation).

Further, for paid family leave taken for the purpose of caring for a newborn or newly adopted child, the Social Security Service grants an allowance equal to the 80 percent of the average daily wage for five months of compulsory leave from work. The parents can ask to be recognized a further period of elective leave from work, and in this case, the allowance granted by INPS is equal to 30 percent of the average daily wage; this further period can go up to a maximum of six months within the third year of the child. Specific provisions withheld in National Collective Bargain Agreements provide that in order to grant the mother (or the father in particular circumstances) 100 percent of the total wage. The remaining part (from 80 percent up to 100 percent of the normal income) has to be paid by the employer.

The period of compulsory maternity leave for women can now be arranged differently. Whereas previously the entitlement was two months prior to confinement and three months after, under the new law, mothers may apply for a period of leave amounting to one month before confinement and four months after.

Additional Leave Costs

The M&A lawyer, whose client is acquiring an Italian company, must include in the due diligence phase, must look at that when a case of personal illness of the employee occurs (illness not covered for by INPS) the paid leave can go up to a year, but single Collective Bargain agreements can allow it for less or more time, depending on the single provisions. In case of illnesses covered for by the Social Security Services, leave can be granted for up to 180 days.

In case of assistance to a relative, the paid leave is granted up to three days per year, but the unpaid leave can be extended up to two years on the whole employment relationship.

In the event of a newborn child or newly adopted, the mother is granted five months of mandatory leave, normally eighth and ninth month of pregnancy and up to the third month of the child. This period can be extended, and the mother can ask for the elective absence from work which, till the third year of the child, can go up to six months of paid leave and after to the third year and up to the eighth year of the child (if occur particular circumstances) up to another four or five months (so, on the whole, no more than 10 or 11 months up to the eighth year of the child). As aforementioned, the elective absence income is granted only up to 30 percent of the average daily wage. Moreover, female workers are entitled to paid time off (*permessi retribuiti*) for prenatal visits and check-ups during working hours.

In case of medical leave due to illness of the child, both mother and father can alternatively ask for unpaid leaves, and can therefore assist him or her through the whole recovery up to the third year of age. On the contrary, between the third year and the eighth year of age, the unpaid leave can only go up to five working days in a row.

Finally, the employer must know that the position has to be held by the company until the return of the employee from family and medical leave. The position does not have to be eliminated in the meantime and the company can replace the absent employee (if absent for long amount of time e.g., over a month) with another but only on a temporary basis, this means until the employee on leave does not return to work. When the employee returns, he or she is granted the same position and tasks. Often companies, in case of parental leave, hire another employee with a fixed-term contract in order to grant covering for the position strictly for a determined period of time equal to the compulsory absence period; that opens up another set of requirements to be explored at another time.

As noted, Italy's parental leave policy designs vary on multiple dimensions. Leave provisions can be, more or less, generous with respect to the amount of total time granted to parents and can be, more or less, generous with respect to the level of financial remuneration provided. One last thing when scrutinizing the Italian "human capital" costs is that female labor market participation varies from one part of the country to another, being much higher in the regions of northern Italy and some central regions than it is in the South.

CHAPTER 8

Target Country—United States—Family Leave Benefits

The U.S. Family and Medical Leave Act (FMLA) sets a minimum standard for parental leave, but due to the exclusion of small employers and short-tenure workers, about 40 percent of U.S. workers are not eligible for the FMLA. In general, U.S. employers, as a group, have not stepped in to fill the gap. While about 60 percent of the workers are eligible for FMLA-related leave, only about one-fourth of the U.S. employers offer fully paid "maternity-related leave" of any duration, and one-fifth of the U.S. employers offer no maternity-related leave of any kind, paid or unpaid. Private employers do not appear to be narrowing the statutory gap in parental leave entitlements between the United States and the rest of the high-income countries analyzed herein.

The United States is the only industrialized nation that does not guarantee workers paid time-off to provide care to a new child, and one of only a handful of these nations that does not provide paid leave for other types of family care.

The FMLA of 1993 was an important accomplishment providing unpaid, job-protected leave to recover from a serious illness, care for a new child, or care for a seriously ill spouse, parent, or child, yet only half of all workers in the United States are covered and eligible. In order to qualify, a worker must have been employed for at least 12 months and worked a minimum of 1,250 hours during that time for an employer with at least 50 employees within a 75-mile radius, which automatically excludes about half of all the workers. Young people and people of color are particularly likely to lack job-protected family and medical leave. Even when workers are eligible for unpaid leave under the FMLA, they often cannot afford to take it. Almost 80 percent of the eligible workers who did not take leave after a qualifying life event said that they would have had it been paid. Because this leave is unpaid, men are less likely to take it to care for a new child than women are. This is both because men tend to earn more than women, and because men often do not think that unpaid leave is intended for them.

Two states, California and New Jersey, recognize the need to make paid family leave available to all workers and have put in place such programs over the past decades. Washington has also passed paid family leave legislation, but it has yet to be implemented. Workers in other states have no guarantee to paid leave unless their employers voluntarily choose to provide it.

Only a small percentage of workers are away from work in an average week for the birth or adoption of a child. In the average week, only 0.4 percent of the workers are out on parental leave. Women are more likely than men to be out of work on parental leave in any given week, which is both because women are more likely than men to take leave, and because women take longer leaves.

Some workers do have access to paid family and medical leave through their workplaces, but because coverage is a voluntary option for employers, it is often offered as a perk for the highest-paid workers. Overall, only about 10 percent of all the workers have access to paid family leave that includes time-off for care-giving. But workers whose average wages are in the lowest 25 percent for their industry are approximately four times less likely to have access to paid family leave than those in the highest 25 percent.

At present, women are more likely than men to leave a job or shift from full-time to part-time work when a new child arrives. Women are also more likely to leave a job or make the shift from full to part-time work in order to provide ongoing care to an elderly, ailing parent. When men are the workers providing family care, however, their working hours decrease as well. Rather than forcing workers to reduce their hours (if that is even possible with their employer) or leave their job altogether, paid family and medical leave would enable these workers to provide care for those in need while still allowing them to return to work once they were able.

Enforcing Family Leave Benefit

The issue of balancing the needs of family life with the desire to have a productive workforce was also addressed by the European Council in 1996 when it adopted the European Union Directive on Parental Leave. The European Directive binds the Member States in some respects as does a traditional law or administrative order. Member States, as a condition to their continued good standing in the European Community, are essentially coerced into compliance. However, the amounts of leave given as well as the methods used to implement and administer the Directive are left up to the individual Member State. Nonetheless, some degree of compliance is required; the source of this requirement is Article 119 of the Treaty of Rome. Article 119 assures employees working in the European Community that both sexes will receive equal pay for comparable work. While there is no express language within Article 119 that demands compliance, both the EC Commission and Parliament have emphasized the importance of uniformity by making and publishing binding decision. In contrast, however, the United States follows no comparable supranational command in its implementation of the FMLA; instead, states are bound by the federal law due to the Constitution and notions of federalism.

Furthermore, as if these consequences are not enough, corporations could be held liable under the U.S. law if they violate U.S. laws while operating abroad. Therefore, it is not likely, but certainly possible, that a multinational operating in Europe could violate not only the relatively employee-favoring provisions of a Member State operating under the Directive, but it could also be held liable for violation of the FMLA in the United States, if the requisite three months of unpaid leave is not given to the employee. Such was the case in *Steele v. Bulova Watch Co.,* which can be analogized to the multinational corporation's dilemma in following the Directive. In *Steele,* an American resident assembled and sold watches in Mexico, bearing a questionable trademark. Under the U.S. law, the U.S. resident was guilty of trademark infringement and unfair competition. The Court focused particularly on the defendant's U.S. nationality, stating, "Congress in prescribing standards of conduct for American citizens may project the impact of its laws beyond the territorial boundaries of the United States." The Court's reasoning identified as light effect on U.S. commerce as a factor in its decision as well.

Similarly, multinational corporations, specifically those originally incorporated in the United States, operating in Europe, who violate the Directive and the FMLA will suffer the consequences in a U.S. tribunal. Such issues have caused some commentators to ask, "What is an American company anymore?" Indeed, others are suggesting an extension of the territorialism of U.S. laws to reach its companies who violate acceptable labor standards on the international level.

In conclusion, the notably shorter and more stringent periods of leave provided for in the FMLA are in sharp contrast to the longer, variable standard the European Union has imposed upon its Member States. The social policies advanced by the respective U.S. and European Union governments are the underlying source of differences in these two approaches. That is, the greater need for employee-protective legislation and the history of a more paternalistic view of employees' rights leads the European Union to impose more restrictions on employers in the Member States in order to extend and preserve employees' rights.

CHAPTER 9

Conclusion—Inadequate Consideration of EC Doctrine and the Relevant Labor Laws in Italy and Germany Can Lead to a Failed Merger and Acquisition

Premerger due diligence in the area of labor law can have a direct impact on the success or failure of merger and acquisition (M&A). The due diligence involving the target country labor laws can help qualify and budget for the necessary severance packages, legal work, and potential fines. Because of the different nuances in labor law in various regions and districts within Germany and Italy, hiring local counsel and not just a U.S. international labor firm is imperative for a successful M&A. The cooperative approach of EC's directive, which provides employees with information prior to merger, and in case of a collective redundancy postmerger, is a foreign concept to U.S. companies. A U.S. company must be prepared for a lengthy collaboration with the work counsel prior obtaining an approval for M&A and also post M&A in a restructuring phase. Strict notice guidelines, compensation packages, legal fees can run into six even seven figures in a scenario involving high-level or long-term employees. Being unaware and unprepared to deal with these costs can compromise a successful M&A.

> The tragedy of America's inability (or unwillingness) to develop the mindset and the mechanisms to compete in this "space between" means that we reduce our options and in the end, resort to the

military instrument. Peace does not exist in a state of inertia. It must be actively and consistently maintained by engaging in the political competitions that are its constant feature.

Most legal scholarship on the work–family intersection has focused on national-level regimes developed to address work–family conflict, such as the U.S. Family and Medical Leave Act (FMLA); yet work–family conflict has an impact that crosses national and cultural boundaries. Joanne Conaghan and Kerry Rittich have pointed out that "negotiating the work/family boundary is…central to the regulatory challenges of the new economy," as maintaining and increasing global productivity depends on harnessing the labor of all workers including the increasing percentage of workers with family.

Clearly, the greatest difference between the FMLA and the EU Directive is the amount of leave given to parents before and after the birth or adoption of a child. The FMLA mandates 12 weeks of unpaid leave to be taken responsibilities within 12 months of the child's birth or adoption, while the typical length of leave granted to European employees is 14 to 16 weeks (though the Directive only requires 12). As aforementioned, the FMLA does not mandate leniency on the part of employers (or to the states implementing these laws) as to how a leave shall be granted; usually, a leave is granted in a single block of time. In contrast, the EU Directive provides considerable leeway for individual nations in enforcement; employers may "divide up" the mandatory leave period in to time before the child's birth and afterward. In addition, Member States have discretion as to whether the leave will be mandated statutorily or by employer–employee agreement.

It's no big secret that the United States is a shameless outlier among our peer nations when it comes to adapting to the realities of the 21st century workforce. Of 168 countries included in a recent global study, 163 guarantee a period of paid leave for childbirth; the United States does not. (Among affluent countries, only the United States and Australia do not provide paid childbirth leave—and Australia offers 52 weeks of job-protected leave to all women, compared to the miserly 12 weeks of unpaid leave available to roughly one-half of women workers in the United States.) While the free market proponents defend this lackadaisical approach as the American way, our nation's abysmal track record on implementing family-friendly polices has led to serious social problems here and will lead to social problems when these same proponents elect to enter the "foreign" arena, as aforementioned.

The social welfare ethic found in European countries is that the upbringing of children is often viewed as a societal responsibility. "The Parental Leave Directive" was the first measure adopted on the basis of a Framework Agreement negotiated between the social partners. The Directive's purpose is to: "facilitate the reconciliation of parental and professional responsibilities for working parents." On the other hand, Americans tend to have an individualistic outlook on life and tend to view the upbringing and care of children "in individual and voluntary terms." Collective responsibility for children is virtually unknown in the United States. The U.S. situation seems to assume that pregnancy (and child rearing to a large extent) is sort of a private hobby, which must be borne at your own expense.

In the United States (more so than elsewhere, including Europe), a vast gulf exists between employment relations law and transactional business law. Yet, of course, those who run U.S. businesses remain acutely aware of the critical role that employment costs play in their enterprises' overall profitability. Total employment costs, including benefits, rival costs of materials as a manufacturing business's chief expense, and usually, far outstrip taxes. (In a service industry, payroll and benefits account for an even greater proportion of total costs.) Yet, notwithstanding this fact of economic life, U.S. transactional business lawyers rarely, if ever, concern themselves with employment issues. Too often, U.S. lawyers negotiating a foreign deal relegate employment issues to the local lawyers to straighten out after closing.

Some explanation for the U.S. "laissez-faire" approach to employees' rights can be gleaned from the already existing statutes such as the Americans with Disabilities Act of 1990 and the Pregnancy Discrimination Act of 1978. One could hypothesize that the less paternalism exists in the United States because there is a smaller need for such laws when antidiscrimination statutes are already in place.

Meanwhile, the more "hands-on approach" of European nations can be traced back to the formation of the actual European Community by the Treaty of Rome of 1957. As early as 1957, Article 119 of the Treaty of Rome sought to protect against sexual discrimination in the workplace, and the Treaty also strived to assure equal pay among the sexes. The European Union's employee-friendly outlook did not come to a halt after the formation of the earliest European Community; instead, the protection of employees has enjoyed a steady progression throughout time, as the European Community Commission has passed several binding decisions and regulations concerning employee protection, including the 1992 Council Directive on pregnancy in the workplace.

The labor-management relations systems in Germany and Italy are largely a product of each nation's individual social, economic, ideological, and political heritage. Each nation has successfully achieved relatively stable labor-management relations, which have contributed to the development of strong national economies.

While these problems seem monumental and confusing to a company beginning their transnational business, steps can be taken to avoid sanctions and maintain the goodwill of their European customers. For example, Coca-Cola Corporation handles its multinational status by having separate divisions. That is, the corporation is divided into local branches by nation. Thus, there is a Coca-Cola of the United States, headquartered in Atlanta, Georgia, and other local branches exist in Italy and France. These local branches fall under the blanket provisions of the Directive; at the same time, Coca-Cola is able to comply with the requirements of the FMLA by having its own separate branch in the United States. Parent companies located in one country, which have foreign-based subsidiaries, are also able to handle the disparity in parental leave standards relatively well. Consider, for example, Daimler Chrysler AG. Located in Germany, Daimler Chrysler's subsidiary company, Mercedes Benz USA LLC is incorporated in Delaware; in addition, Mercedes has a manufacturing plant housed in Vance, Alabama. Of course, Daimler Chrysler itself need not worry about its own employees housed in Germany; such workers are subject to Germany's version of the European Union Directive. Naturally, since Mercedes, though a subsidiary of Daimler Chrysler is incorporated in the United States, it is subject to the provisions of the FMLA and must follow the U.S. statutory guidelines. Another way then for companies to easily comply with both standards is to reincorporate as a subsidiary in a foreign country.

In summary, family leave is an important issue in the United States and in Europe, as exemplified by the passage of the FMLA and the Directive. While the United States and the European Community share the same purpose in promoting these laws, namely to grant parents adequate leave time to spend with children, their guidelines and flexibility are very different. The FMLA governs all U.S. states and allows for 12 weeks of unpaid leave, to be taken with 12 months of the birth or adoption of a child. In contrast, the Directive gives employees the same three-month period of leave, but allows Member States to alter or extend the period so long as they meet the minimum requirement. This disparity results in a major international difference when it comes to family leave. Even across the European Union, there are major differences; some leave is granted by statute, other is by employer contract. These differences result in a severe lack of uniformity across Europe and across the world when determining how much family leave an employee may take and what the conditions of that leave are.

To combat such problems and because of the varying standards, it is imperative that drastic measures be taken. The question remains: how much due diligence and to what extent would U.S. corporations go to incorporate aspects of foreign industrial relations systems into its own system? Especially without "golden guarantees"! This is a question worthy of consideration.

Beware—the cultural divide between countries that may well create major issues to hinder business integrations, with no impossible scenarios, just situations that require more education and investigation. In the world of M&As, it is clear that U.S. investors investing in a foreign country need to get the right picture of the courts, laws, and customs before "spending the green."

The following is a suggested checklist for the legal and HR team to implement when contemplating a merger or acquisition in EU, with specific attention given to Italy and Germany.

1. *Include HR in the deal from the beginning of M&A contemplation*: It is crucial that HR is part of the deal team along with corporate, tax, benefits, and stock option specialist in order to avoid HR nightmares due to unfeasible timelines, confusion about what the acquisition agreement requires, lack of understanding about how the corporate structure influences employee transfers, and other issues.

2. *Coordinate between various integration teams*: Corporate and tax planning teams need to clear HR and business teams before any informal integration is planned of foreign subsidiaries. There can be significant consequences in foreign jurisdictions if the structure is not permitted by local tax authorities.

3. *Address works council, employee representatives, and union requirements*: In EU and particularly in Germany and Italy, works council, employee representatives, or unions have significant powers; thus, companies should allow for significant time to understand the works council, employee representative, or union situation, prepare for it, and fully comply with the consultation process.

4. *Analyze and plan the employee transfer method*: It is crucial for employment lawyers and members of the HR team to understand the appropriate employee transfer method and abide by various notice requirements, consultation requirements, and severance considerations.

5. *Analyze and understand limitations and cost of redundancies*: At-will employment is virtually nonexistent outside of the United States. Instead, most jurisdictions around the world require not only notice and severance, but also cause to terminate an employment relationship. A redundancy triggered by duplication of roles after an acquisition will often not suffice. Business transfers in European Union Member States are not viewed as grounds for dismissal of employees.

6. *Understand terms and conditions of employment and how their significance in an M&A*: The European Union's Acquired Rights Directive (EUARD) requires that employees transfer with their existing terms and conditions of employment. Some jurisdictions of EU will not recognize a mutually agreed upon modification of terms (between employer and employee) and even go so far as to invalidate them. Before any monetary compensation is offered as consideration for modification, the EUARD must be addressed.

7. *Understand employee classifications and the regulations pertaining to wage, hours, and benefits*: Misclassification of employees can be extremely expensive if compensatory damages are assessed.

8. *Plan in time for benefit transfers*: The existence of various policies and plans, both statutory and contractual, that have to be terminated,

transferred, realigned can cause a significant delay in benefit transfers, which in turn can cause a legal liability for HR.

9. *Understand labor market regulations*: Working hours, employment protection, dismissal protection, employment forms, wage agreements, industrial action, job placement, codetermination, notice requirements, privacy.

10. *Understand the laws and regulations behind agreement enforceability*: In the United States, employers often require noncompete agreements. In various EU jurisdictions, Germany for example, in order for a noncompete to be enforceable, there must be consideration. A job itself does not take place of consideration.

11. *Immigration*: Target country immigration laws, processing time, and requirements and cost.

12. *Local representation*: Hire local legal counsel, industrial relations consultant, and talent acquisition consultant to address legal regulations and requirements, risk analysis, human capital availability, cultural challenges.

13. *Know the appropriate labor-governing bodies*: EU, national, and local work councils, trade unions. Labor unions, employee representatives, and their powers.

14. *Research discrimination laws*: Verify compliance with local discrimination, diversity, and harassment laws including laws on pay equity, affirmative action, mandatory training, and "bullying."

15. *Research privacy laws*: Stringent personal and data privacy laws may impede employee data transfer and slow down the HR transition process.

16. Identify the cultural difference and similarities between home corporation and target country.

Bibliography

Cases

Case C-281197, *Kruger v. KreiskrankenhausEbersburg*, Official Journal C 352 (1999).

Case C-207/98, *Silke-Kurin Mahlburg v. Land Mecklenburg-Vorpominem*, Feb. 3, 2000.

Case C-226/98, *Birgitte Jorgensen v. Foreningen af SpecillWger and Sygesikringens Forhandlingsuvalg*, Apr. 6, 2000, at https://europa.eu/

Christopher v. SmithKline Beecham Corp., 132 S.Ct. 2156 (2012).

Collino & Chiappero v. Telecom Italia SpA, 2000 E.C.R. I-6659.

Commission v. Belgium, Case 215/83, [1985] E.C.R. 1039, [1985] 3 C.M.L.R. 624.

Electromation, Inc. v. NLRB, Nos. 92-4129, 93-1169 (7th Cir. 1994).

Finnan v. L.F. Rothschild & Co., 726 F. Supp. 460 (S.D.N.Y. 1989).

Jones v. Kayser-Roth Hosiery, Inc., 748 F. Supp. 1276 (E.D. Tenn. 1990).

Local 397 v. Midwest Fasteners, Inc., 763 F. Supp. 78 (D.N.J. 1990).

Steele v. Bulova Watch Co., 344 U.S. 280 (1952).

Statutes

29 U.S.C. § 2102 (1988).

29 U.S.C. § 2103(2) (1988).

29 U.S.C. § 8 et. Seq.

29 U.S.C. §§ 151–169.

29 U.S.C. §§ 2101–2109 (1988).

Family and Medical Leave Act of 1993, H.R. 1, 103rd Congress (1993).

FMLA 29 U.S.C. §§ 2601–2654 (2012).

Family and Medical Leave Act of 1993, 29 U.S.C. §§ 2601–2654 (1994).

WARN Act 29 U.S.C. §§ 2101 to 2109.

Transcript of Congressional Hearing

Brown, Hon. Sherrod, a U.S. Senator from the State of Ohio, HEARING OF THE COMMITTEE ON HEALTH, EDUCATION, LABOR, AND PENSIONS UNITED STATES SENATE.

Constitutional Provisions

The Economic Dislocation and Worker Adjustment Assistance Act (EDWAA) amended Title III of the Job Training Partnership Act (JTPA), U.S. CONST. AMEND. X.

Regulations

20 C.F.R. § 639.3(h) (1991).

Bureau of Labor Statistics, Table 2. Wage and Salary Workers Who Took Leave from their Main Job. During an Average Week: percent of Workers Taking Leave, Hours of Leave Taken and Type of Leave Used; Main reason for taking leave 2011.

Dept. of Labor (2012).

International Statutes, Directives, Policy

Bundeselterngeld-und Elternzeitgesetz of December 5, 2006.

Commission Proposal for a Council Directive on Parental Leave and Leave for Family Reasons, art. JI, 1983 O.J. (C 333) 6.

Council Directive 96/34/EC 1960.

Family Benefits, INPS; EURAXESS Italy, European Commission—Employment, Social Affairs and Equal Opportunities; Your Europe—Family; Eurofound; www.welcomeoffice.fvg.it/

Maternity Leave and Job Protection (Mutterschutz) in Germany, Federal Ministry for Family, Seniors, Women & Adolescents, Maternity Protection Guide. (September 2005).

OECD. *Gender Brief.* Prepared by the OECD Social Policy Division. Version: March 2010.

Office of Retirement and Disability Policy, *Social Security Programs Throughout the World: Europe, 2012.* www.ssa.gov/policy/docs/progdesc/ssptw/2012-2013/europe/italy.html

Treaty Establishing the European Economic Community, Mar. 25, 1957, art. 119, 298, U.N.T.S. 42.

Italian Law

www.ilo.org/global/lang--en/index.htm

In Italy, Law No. 628 of 1961.

The freedom of association (Libertà sindacale) is based on Article 39 of the Italian Constitution.

Law Review

"Germany Country Summary." 2004. Columbia University: The Clearinghouse on International Developments in Child, Youth, and Family Policies. Retrieved October 24, 2006 from www.childpolicyintl.org

Hyde, A. 1986. "Rights for Canadian Members of International Unions Under the U.S. Labor-Management Reporting and Disclosure Act." *Wash. L. Rev.* 61, pp. 1007, 1015.

Angestelltenbetriebstrat der Wiener GebietSkrankenkasse and Wiener Gebietskrankenkasse, 1999 E.C.R. 1-2907

Pelletier, A. 2006–2007. "The Family Medical Leave Act of 1993-Why Does Parental Leave in the United States Fall so Far Behind Europe?" *Gonz. L. Rev.* 42, p. 547.

Pelletier, A. 2006. "The Family Medical Leave Act of 1993-Why Does Parental Leave in the United States Fall so Far Behind Europe?" *Gonz. L. Rev.* 42, p. 547.

Grill, A.H. 1996. "The Myth of Unpaid Family Leave: Can the United States Implement a Paid Leave Policy Based on the Swedish Model?" *17 Comp. Lab. L.J.* p. 373.

(citing HR 2020, 99th Cong. [1st Sess.1985]).

Block, R.N, P. Berg, and K. Roberts. Forthcoming. "Comparing and Quantifying Labour Standards in the United States and the European Union." *International and Comparative Journal of Labour Law and Industrial Relations*, School of Labor & Industrial Relations, Michigan State University, September 19, 2003.

Block, R.N., P. Berg, and D. Belman. 2004. "The Economic Dimension of the Employment Relationship." In *The Employment Relationship: Examining Psychological and Contextual Perspectives*, eds. J. Coyle-Shapiro, L. Shore, S. Taylor, and L. Tetrick. Oxford, UK: Oxford University Press.

McCaffrey, C.A., and A. Graff. 1999. "European Union Directive on Parental Leave: Will the European Union Face the Same Problems as Those Faced by the United States Under the 1993 Family and Medical Leave Act." *Hofstra Lab. & Emp. L.J* 17, pp. 229–230.

Rasnic, C.D. 1994. "United States' 1993 Family and Medical Leave Act: How Does It Compare with Work Leave Laws in European countries?" *The Conn. J. Int'l* L 10, p. 105.

Carol, K. 1989. *On Family Leave Plans U.S. is Left Far Behind.* CHI. TRIB., May 22, § 4 at 2.

Alewell, D., and K. Pull. 2000. *An International Comparison and Assessment of Maternity Leave Regulations.* University of Jena. www.wiwi.uni-jena.de/Papers/wp-a0102.pdf

Dowling, D.C., Jr. 1993. "EC Employment Law After Maastricht: 'Continental Social Europe.'" *The International Lawyer* 27, no. 1, pp. 1–26.

Gereffi, G. 1996. "Community Chains and Regional Divisions of Labor in East Asia." *Journal of Asian Business* 12, no. 1, pp. 75, 81.

Drummonds, H.H. 2000. "Transnational Small and Emerging Business in a World of Nikes and Microsoft." *J. Small & Emerging Bus L* 4, p. 249.

Horwitz, F.M., K. Anderssen, A. Bezuidenhout, S. Cohen, F. Kirsten, K. Mosoeunyane, N. Smith, K. Thole, and A. Van Heerden. 2002. "Due Diligence Neglected: Managing Human Resources and Organizational Culture in Mergers and Acquisitions." *NSA Journal of Business Management* 33.

Parry, J.A. 2001. "Family Leave Policies: Examining Choice and Contingency in Industrial Nations." *NWSA Journal* 13, no. 3, pp. 70–94.

Cavens, M.J. 1983. "Japanese Labor Relations and Legal Implications of Their Possible Use in the United States." *Northwestern Journal of International Law & Business* 5, p. 585.

Adams, K.L. 2014. "The Family Responsibilities Convention Reconsidered: The Work-Family Intersection in International Law Thirty Years On." *Introduction to Labour Law, Work, and Family*, eds. J. Conaghan and K. Rittich. *Cardozo J. of Int'l & Comp Law* 22, p. 201.

Morris, K.L. 2001. "A Matter of Compliance: How Do U.S. Multinational Corporations Deal with the Discrepancies in the Family and Medical Leave Act of 1993 and the European Union Directive on Parental Leave; is an International Standard Practical or appropriate in this area of law?" *Ga. J. Int'l & Comp. L* 30, p. 543.

Kolvenbach, W. 1981. "Co-Determination in Germany: History and Practical Experience." *Int'l Bus. Law* 9, p. 163.

Lefkoe, P. 1987. "Why So Many Mergers Fail." *Fortune*, July 20.

DiMaggio, M. September 15, 2009. The Top 10 Best (and Worst) Corporate Mergers of All Time … or, the Good, the Bad, and the Ugly." *Rasmussen College Blog*. www.rasmussen.edu/degrees/business/blog/best-and-worst-corporate-mergers

Houser, L., and T.P. Vartanian. 2012. *The Positive Economic Impact of Paid Family Leave for Families, Businesses and the Public*, State University of N.J. Found on Internet at Key Paid Family Leave/Paid Family and Medical Leave Research.

Brody, D.H., P.S. Bryant, T.T. Crouch, and L.L. Rippey. 1998. "Alternatives to the United States System of Labor Relations: A Comparative Analysis of the Labor Relations Systems in the Federal Republic of Germany, Japan and Sweden." *Vand. L. Rev* 41, p. 627.

Mabry, L.A. 1999. "Multinational Corporations and U.S. Technology Policy: Rethinking the Policy of Corporate Nationality." *Geo. L.J* 81, p. 563.

Meller, P. 2003. "Europe Accuses Microsoft of Continuing Antitrust Abuses." *The New York Times*, August 6.

Schuchmann, M.L. 1995. "The Family and Medical Leave Act of 1993: A Comparative Analysis with Germany." *J. Corp. L* 20, pp. 331, 335.

Schuchmann, M.L. 1995. "The Family and Medical Leave Act of 1993: A Comparative Analysis with Germany." *Iowa J. Corp. L* 20, p. 331.

O'Reilly, C. 1998. "*Cisco Systems: The Acquisition of Technology Is the Acquisition of People.* Case HR 10. Graduate School of Business, Stanford University.

Hicks, P., and D. Westbrook. August 2013. "Family and Medical Leave Pointers for the General Practitioner: FMLA: It's Not Just for Employment Lawyers Anymore." *Nev. Law.* 12.

Thompson, P., T. Wallace, and J. Flecker. 1992. "The Urge to Merge: Organizational Change in the Merger and Acquisitions Process in Europe." *International Journal of Human Resource Management* 3, no. 2, pp. 285–306.

Fass, S. 2009. *Paid Leave in the States: A critical Support for Low-wage Workers and Their Families.* National Center for Children in Poverty, Columbia University.

Summers, C. 1984. "Worker Participation in Sweden and the United States: Some Comparisons from an American Perspective." *University of Pennsylvania Law Review* 133, p. 175, 202.

"The Real German Model." *Wall Street Journal*, January 16, 1995.

"Tips for Companies Operating in the EU." *Eurowatch, Employment* 8, no. 8, June 10, 1996.

Rinne, U., and K.F. Zimmermann. 2013. "Is Germany the North Star of Labor Market Policy?" *IMF Economic Review* 61, no. 4, pp. 702–29.

Weber, R.P. 1990. *Basic Content Analysis.* Boston: Harvard University Press

Winestock, G. 2001. "ED Threatens WTO Steel Suits Against U.S. by End of Month." *The Wall Street Journal*, June 12.

Articles

Wright, A.D. June 30, 2010. "Successful Mergers Integrate Cultures." SHRM Publications. www.shrm.org/hr-today/news/hr-news/pages/successfulmergers integratecultures.aspx

Delaney, A. 2014. "Paid Maternity Leave Push Underway at U.S. Labor Department." *Huff Post, Politics*, September 30.

Atkinson, P., and D. Clarke. 2007. "Conducting a Pre-Acquisition Investigation." Integrating Culture & Technology for Rapid Growth. www.philipatkinson. com/uploads/7/1/5/0/7150143/developing_a_cultural_audit_for_post_ acquistion_integration_-_philip_atkinson_&_dara_clarke.pdf

Birkinshaw, J., H. Bresman, and L. Hakanson. 2000. "Managing the Post-Acquisition Integration Process." *Journal of Management Studies* 37, no. 3, pp. 395–425.

Cartwright, S., and C.L. Cooper. 1996. *Managing Mergers, Acquisitions and Strategic Alliances: Integrating People and Culture.* London-Butterworth-Heinemann, Ltd.

Bohlen, C. 1996. "The State of Welfare in Italy; Where Every Day Is Mother's Day." *The New York Times,* May 12.

Charman, A. 1999. "Global Mergers and Acquisitions: The Human Resource Challenge" International Focus (Society for Human Resource Management).

Jacobsen, D. 2012. "6 Big Mergers that Were Killed by Culture (and How to Stop It from Killing Yours)." *Globoforce* (blog home page). www.globoforce.com/gfblog/2012/6-big-mergers-that-were-killed-by-culture

Weiss, D.A. n.d. "Opening in a Foreign Country; Be Careful." *Global Business News.*

Tim, D. 2013. "Republicans Slam Administration Over WARN Act Waivers" *The Washington Times,* February 14.

Dinh, V.D. 1999. "Codetermination and Corporate Governance in a Multinational Business Enterprise." *Journal of Corporate Law* 24, p. 975.

James, D., and E. Steve. 2014. "Without Warning: Effects and Reform of the WARN Act" *The Blade,* October 19.

Dundon, T., and P.J. Gollan. 2007. "Reconceptualising Voice in the Non-Union Workplace." *The International Journal of Human Resource Management* 18, no. 7, pp. 1182–98.

Elwin. 2010. "Mergers and Acquisitions Failures Are Project Management Failures." www.tobyelwin.com/mergers-and-acquisitions-failures-are-project-management–failures

Horwitz, F.M., K. Anderssen, A. Bezuidenhout, S. Cohen, F. Kirsten, K. Mosoeunyane, N. Smith, K. Thole, and A. Van Heerden. 2002. "Due Diligence Neglected: Managing Human Resources and Organizational Culture in Mergers and Acquisitions." ÑSA Journal of Business Managementî 33.

Fisher, L.M. 1998. "Post-Merger Integration on How Novartis Became No. 1." *Strategy Business* no. 11, pp. 70–78.

Floyd, M. 1991. "The Scope of Assistance for Dislocated Workers in the United States and the European Community: WARN and Directive 75/129 Compared." *Fordham Int'l L.J* 15, p. 436.

Frick, B., M.A. Malo, P. Garcia, and M. Schneider. 2012. "The Demand for Individual Grievance Procedures in Germany and Spain: Labour Law Changes versus Business Cycle." *Estudios De Economia Aplicada* 30, no. 1, pp. 12–28.

Friederike, G., M. Kappenhagen, and G. Mikes. March, 2014. "Labor and Employment Law Projects of the New German Government." *Jones Day Commentary.*

Schweiger, D.M., and Y. Weber. 1990. *Innovation in Manufacturing Industry.* London: HMSO.

Farrell, J., and J. Venator. 2012. "Paid Family and Medical Leave; Updated Labor Standards Could Help U.S. Workers Make Ends Meet." *Center for American Progress*, August 16.

Krugman, P. 2001. "The Price of Good Mergers is Eternal Vigilance." *The Straits Times*, January 16.

Speer, L.J. February 3, 2000. "International Agreements: OECD Revising Guidelines for Multinationals; Environment, Labor Standards Prominent." BNA International Trade Report.

Matteis, A., P. Accardo, and G. Mammone. June 17, 2011. "National Labour Law Profile: Italy."

Maurer, R. 2009. "Why Most Mergers Fail: Global employment Law Compliance; Complex Differences Can Cause Headaches FOR Even Seasoned in-House Counsel." N.Y.L.J (online), September 14.

Muhl, C.J. 2001. "The Employment-at-Will Doctrine: Three Major Exceptions." *Monthly Labor Review* 124, pp. 3–11.

Mutterschutzgesetz [MuSchG]. 1994. Bundesgesetzblatt [BGBIJ 1 1170 (Germany).

Atkinson, P., and D. Clarke. n.d. "Integrating Culture & Technology for Rapid Growth." Woburn Consulting Group.

Price, L. 1999. "Helping People Stay on Their Feet During Mergers and Acquisitions." *People Dynamics* 17, pp. 36–42.

Ray, R., G. Equality, J.C. Gornick, and J. Schmitt. 2008. "Parental Leave Policies in 21 Countries, Assessing Generosity and Gender Equality." Center for Economic and Policy Research. Revised June, 2009.

Ray, R., J.C. Gornick, and J. Schmitt. 2008. "Parental Leave Policies in 21 Countries." Center for Economic and Policy Research (cepr), Revised June 2009.

Rottig, D. 2007. "Successfully Managing International Mergers And Acquisitions: A Descriptive Framework." *The Journal of the AIB-SE* 1, no. 1, pp. 103–26.

Schweiger, D.M., and Weber, K. 1990 "Strategies for Managing Human Resources during Mergers and Acquisitions: An Empirical Investigation Select Committee on Science and Technology (1991)." *Human Resource Planning* 12, no. 2, pp. 69–86.

Soros, G. January 1998. "Toward a Global Open Society." *The Atlantic Monthly* 281, no. 1, pp. 20–32.

Stone, K.V.W. 2007. "Revisiting the at-Will Employment Doctrine: Imposed Terms, Implied Terms, and the Normative World of the Workplace." *Industrial Law Journal* 36, no. 1, pp. 84–101.

Strauss, G. 2006. "Worker Participation—Some Under-Considered Issues." *Industrial Relations Journal* 45, no. 4, pp. 778–803.

Tetenbaum, T.J. 1999. "Beating the Odds of Merger and Acquisition Failure: Seven Key Practices that Improve the Chance for Expected Integration and Synergies." *Organizational Dynamics* 28, no. 2, pp. 22–36.

Woburn Update: "Integrating Culture & Technology for Rapid Growth." Woburn Consulting Group. www.woburnconsulting.com

Zakson, L.S. 1984. "Worker Participation: Industrial Democracy and Managerial Prerogative in the Federal Republic of Germany, Sweden and the United States." *Hastings Int'l and Comp. L. Rev* 8, p. 93, 114.

Books

Bloomberg BNA. 2012. International Labor and Employment Laws, at 1, 4th ed., The European Union (3rd ed.).

Bloomberg BNA. 2014. International Labor and Employment Laws, 4th ed., Italy (3rd).

Farnsworth, E.A. 1990. Contracts § 8.15, 2nd ed.

Bloomberg BNA. 2014. International Labor and Employment Laws, 4th ed., Germany, (3rd ed.).

Shane and Rosenthal. 1999. *Employment Law Deskbook*, § 16.02.

Publications

Dowling, D.C., Jr. September 2012. "Global HR Topic—September 2012: Employment-Context Choice-of-Law Clauses." White & Case LLP Publications.

H.R. CONF. REP. No. 576, 100th Cong., 2d Sess., reprinted in 1988 U.S.C.C.A.N. 2082.

Herbert, G. 2003. "Administrative Justice in Europe–Report for Germany." Association of the Councils of State and Supreme Administrative Jurisdictions of the European Union. Retrieved May 6, 2014.

Consultation

Consultation with Edel Revord of Mercedes-Benz U.S. International Inc. HRM/T with consultation in German from Gabriele Weber.

Consultation with Elena Ghigo, Jonson and Johnson Italy.

Jeffrey A. Van Detta, Associate Dean, Atlanta's John Marshall Law School.

EU Directive

Council Directive No. 75/129, OJ. L 48/29 (1975).

EU Directive 94/45.

EU Directives 75/129 and 92/56.

EU Directives 77/187 and 98/50.

EU Directives 80–391, 89/391/EEC, 89/654/EEC, 89/655/EEC, 89/656/EEC, 90/269/EEC, 90/270/EEC, 90/394/EEC, and 90/679/EEC.

Proposal to Close Loophole in Collective Redundancies Directive.

Interviews

Davis, B., and A. Raghavan. 2001. "Consumers vs. Competition: U.S., Europe Depend on Circumstances to Choose Sides." *The Wall Street Journal*, July 3.

Interview with Elena Ghigo of Johnson and Johnson International (Italy Division), (July, 2014).

Interview with Prof. Jeffrey A. Van Detta, at John Marshall School of Law, Atlanta, GA.

Shiskin, P. 2001. "EU Officially Blocks GE-Honeywell Deal." *The Wall Street Journal*, July 5.

Web Page

European Industrial Relations Observatory: www.eurofound.europa.eu/observatories/eurwork

Marco Trentini and Ires Lombardia, *New law adopted on parental leave,* Eironline [European industrial relations observatory on line] (Oct. 1999) The European Union, at www. europa.eu.int/abc-en.htm (last visited Oct. 3, 2000). Welfare State, *Wikipedia* http://en.wikipedia.org/wiki/Welfare_state

Treaty

Article 48, Treaty of Rome.

Treaty Establishing the European Economic Community, Mar. 25, 1957.

German Civil Code

§ 1(1) KSchG, the termination with notice of an employment relationship that has existed for more than six months is legally invalid when it is "socially unjustified" (this term is defined in detail in § 1(2) and (3) KSchG).

Bürgerliches Gesetzbuch (BGB) (German Civil Code) of 18 August 1896 [RGBl. I S. 195,III 4.

Bürgerliches Gesetzbuch (BGB) (German Civil Code) of 18 August 1896 [RGBl. I S. 195,III 4 Nr. 400-2], as amended in the version promulgated on 2 January 2002 (Federal Law Gazette [*Bundesgesetzblatt*] I page 42, 2909; 2003 I page 738), last amended by Article 4 para. 5 of the Act of 1 October 2013 (Federal Law Gazette I page 3719) Title 8, Subtitle 1 Section 623 Termination of employment by notice of termination or separation agreement requires written form to be effective; electronic form is excluded.

Bürgerliches Gesetzbuch (BGB) (German Civil Code) Section 622. www. bundesregierung.de

Termination Protection Act [Kündigungsschutzgesetz; KSchG], in the version of the Proclamation of 25 August 1969 [BGBl. I, p. 1317].

Termination Protection Statute, Section 1(1).

Termination Protection Statute, Section 23(1), Sentences 3 and 4.

Definitions

Dismissal for economic or reorganization reasons (objective reasons, such as the suppression of job position).

European Court of Justice (created in in 1952 as the Court of Justice of the European Coal and Steel Communities) later named Court of Justice of the European Communities.

European Works Councils.

Germany has a two-tier board there is an executive board (all executive directors) and a separate supervisory board (all non-executive directors) which was created to provide a monitoring role over corporate governance.

In the mid-1950s, 36% of the United States labor force was unionized.

Labor Legislation

The Civil Code adopted on 18.08.1896 and last amended on 02.11.2000.

The European Court of Human Rights (ECtHR; French: *Cour européenne des droits de l'homme*) is a supra-national or international court established by the European Convention on Human Rights.

Upon dismissal for any reason, employees in Italy are entitled to the "*Trattamento di Fine Rapporto*" ("*T.F.R.*"). "*T.F.R.*"

When a collective bargaining agreement is involved, the method for determining the applicable notice period for termination is different.

German Statute

Basic Law–Article 9 Paragraph 3.
www.eurofound.europa.eu/emire/GERMANY/WORKSCONSTITUTION-
    DE.htm: Works Constitution Act (Betriebsverfassungsgesetz) of 1972
www.ilo.org/ National Labour Law Profile: Federal Republic of Germany
www.ilo.org/ Source IAB Betriebspanel
www.ilo.org/ifpdial/information-resources/national-labour-law-profiles

Index

OTHER TITLES IN OUR BUSINESS LAW COLLECTION
John Wood, Econautics Sustainability Institute, Editor

- *Preventing Litigation: An Early Warning System to Get Big Value out of Big Data* by Nelson E. Brestoff and William H. Inmon
- *Light on Peacemaking: A Guide to Appropriate Dispute Resolution and Mediating Family Conflict* by Thomas DiGrazia
- *Understanding Consumer Bankruptcy: A Guide for Businesses, Managers, and Creditors* by Scott B. Kuperberg
- *The History of Economic Thought: A Concise Treatise for Business, Law, and Public Policy* by Robert Ashford and Stefan Padfield

Business Expert Press has over 30 collection in business subjects such as finance, marketing strategy, sustainability, public relations, economics, accounting, corporate communications, and many others. For more information about all our collections, please visit www.businessexpertpress.com/collections.

Business Expert Press is actively seeking collection editors as well as authors. For more information about becoming an BEP author or collection editor, please visit http://www.businessexpertpress.com/author

Announcing the Business Expert Press Digital Library
Concise e-books business students need for classroom and research

This book can also be purchased in an e-book collection by your library as

- a one-time purchase,
- that is owned forever,
- allows for simultaneous readers,
- has no restrictions on printing, and
- can be downloaded as PDFs from within the library community.

Our digital library collections are a great solution to beat the rising cost of textbooks. E-books can be loaded into their course management systems or onto students' e-book readers.
The **Business Expert Press** digital libraries are very affordable, with no obligation to buy in future years. For more information, please visit **www.businessexpertpress.com/librarians**. To set up a trial in the United States, please email **sales@businessexpertpress.com**.